AF423973

Enlighten

An artful, heartful poetry collection

and chakra journey, inviting you

to learn, laugh, love, live and lift your spirit!

Sonya Bhalla

ISBN (paperback) 978-9948-758-70-9

COPYRIGHT NOTICE

As a writer I have a lot to say,
and being a lawyer by day
here comes the legal terms of use
to prevent copyright abuse.
So, please take heed;
there's really no need
to copy any of my work,
it's purely for your pleasure,
to read at your leisure.

All and any part of my poems, quotes,
prose, pictures, designs and notes;
basically, anything I create and write
are my copyright,
from the moment each piece was born
in any form,
format and frame
under my social and real name.

Please don't remove my name or references
to my ownership from any material,
as copyright infringement is not trivial.
Please respect my rights as outlined here
and check what is permissible
if anything remains unclear.

DEDICATION

To my late father, who gave me lots of inspiration to write and always encouraged an inquisitive mind. His love of books and aspiration to publish rubbed off on me. I hope I have fulfilled his wish. I would like him to know that wherever he is, he is loved, missed, and lives on in our hearts, thoughts, and my writing.

To my amazing mum who has encouraged me to keep writing, and to follow my heart and passion. Your humility, sincerity, abundant love, and selfless heart continues to grace all our lives. Thank you.

To my wonderful children who have given me lots of inspiration too. I love you dearly, from infinity and beyond and forever more. I hope you enjoy the poems and read them whenever you are lost, feeling inquisitive or looking for some positive vibes in your life. I appreciate that a lot of it won't make sense now in your younger years, but I hope that one day it will instil some food for thought in the future.

To my dearest husband who sometimes may not be on the same page but continues to be my book spine and his loving support binds us together.

CONTENTS

COPYRIGHT NOTICE 5

DEDICATION 7

ACKNOWLEDGEMENTS 13

PREFACE 14

INTRODUCTION 17

The Write Vibe 18

Poetry Is … 19

CHAKRA ONE 21

The Root Chakra 21

Global Garden 24

Family Tree 25

Defining Lines 30

Gaia 35

The Five Elements 39

Decoding Nature 43

Our Mother Earth 49

Sand Dunes 53

Home Improvements 54

Life Audit – A Checklist 59

CHAKRA TWO 65

The Sacral Chakra 65

Embryonic Universe 68

Winter Solstice 72

Sandstorms... 77

Gabber Napper 78

Misunderstanding 82

Snowdrops.. 86

Happiness 88

The Universal Language of Laughter 90

Creative Energy 94

CHAKRA THREE 97

The Solar Plexus Chakra 97

Patchwork Quilt.. 100

Mirror Lake 103

Puzzle Piece 104

Life's Purpose 109

Make-up Routine.. 113

Ambition.. 118

Life's Lessons 119

CHAKRA FOUR 123

The Heart Chakra... 123

Motherhood 126

Valentine's Card 131

Phases of the Moon.. 135

Beware = Be + Aware 136

Unpleasant Emotions 137

Resilience 141

Heartbeat.. 143

CHAKRA FIVE... 145

The Throat Chakra 145

Balance of Scales 148

Perspective 150

The Sound of Music 153

Sonic Tonic.. 158

Bubbles 161

Tumbling Words 162

Artistic Visions 164

CHAKRA SIX 171

The Third Eye Chakra.................................... 171

Spring.. 174

Dream Catcher... 176

Instinct 178

Kaleidoscope.. 179

Conspiracy Theory 182

Bindi.. 183

Behind Our Eyes 185

Escape 188

CHAKRA SEVEN 193

The Crown Chakra 193

Ancient Art Forms.. 196

Memories 200

The Water Cycle 201

Lotus 204

A Soul's Journey.. 209

Stardust & Starlight 210

ALL CHAKRAS & BEYOND.................................. 215

Sunset 217

Reframe 218

Layers... 220

Life is a Stage 221

Russian Dolls.. 222

Abundant Affirmations..................................... 225

Manifesting Wishes 226

Enlighten.. 227

AUTHOR'S NOTE 229

ABOUT THE AUTHOR 231

ACKNOWLEDGEMENTS

I wish to thank all the scientists, scholars, and influencers who have imparted so much positivity, knowledge and interesting perspectives.

I have learnt so much from reading all sorts of wide-ranging material, some rationally insightful and some just wonderfully weird.

I also wish to thank my wonderful editor Sage Taylor Kingsley who has weaved her magic through the fabric of my poetic pieces.

I would also like to thank my besties - you know who you are ;-) and my beta readers including my mum, who have supported and encouraged me to complete this long overdue collection.

PREFACE

My poetry collection mainly covers life's experiences and topics everyone can relate to such as motherhood, pregnancy, happiness, belonging, escape, dreams, and more. However, the majority seek to include a positive vibe, or spiritual outlook to life and our experiences.

Throughout my life, I have always had an innate belief in a higher purpose and a feeling that there is so much more to us that we have yet to discover.

Over the years I have been drawn towards everything spiritual, and intrigued by new scientific findings, the benefits of meditation, yoga, chakras, sound healing and other ancient wisdom, which still have a place and purpose today, allowing us to find out who we are, our place and our life goals.

My poems and prose are therefore centred around the spiritual aspects of life, based around common themes around body, mind, soul and spirit. They also seek to explore spiritual mysteries and theories beyond our physical realm.

My poems are split into chapters covering each of the different chakras and what they represent in our life and how energy flows through each one until we reach enlightenment. Although there are thirteen chakras or more, I have divided this collection among the seven well known main chakras.

I have also included my own illustrations throughout the collection to coincide with many of the pieces.

For more detailed information about the chakras, what happens physically and emotionally when they are unbalanced, and how to align them, there are many comprehensive books which can help.

I have drawn inspiration and information from the many documentaries, articles and other literature I have gleaned over the years. These poems are my thoughts and perspectives and I appreciate there may be differing views, or I may have misunderstood some scientific aspects. Afterall, poetry involves the freedom to express ourselves and be creative.

Overall, this collection will appeal to anyone who is interested in the mysteries of life, our spirit, soul, and our place in the Universe.

INTRODUCTION

"Poetry is not only dream and vision;
it is the skeleton architecture of our lives.
It lays the foundations for a future of change,
a bridge across our fears
of what has never been before."
Audre Lorde

The Write Vibe

Creating the write vibe
about life, our experiences
is my reason to transcribe
my reflections
on what it means
to be truly alive.

May my musings
resonate,
motivate,
instil goodness,
kindness,
hope and happiness.

May they
help you create
a fulfilling life
of self-awareness
and be a prelude
for enlightened
consciousness.

Poetry Is ...

an array of birds flying high
like sparse words
and soaring thoughts
flocking together in cloudy skies
to feel the warmth of the Sun,
see the rays of light,
and hear the whispers of the wise.

CHAKRA ONE

The Root Chakra

"Nature is the source of all true knowledge."

Leonardo Da Vinci

The Root Chakra

The Root Chakra (known as *Muladhara*) is the base or foundation on which the rest of the chakras connect and build upon after the Earth Star. It therefore represents stability, survival, and the basic needs necessary to live within our material world. This includes our material and emotional needs, and comforts as we navigate our lives. It's all about supporting our roots.

The mantra "*I am* ..." points to this chakra reflecting our identity as individuals, our self-awareness, and self-development. Together, these qualities allow us to learn, improve and evolve.

In this chapter, the "*I AM*" is rooted in a worldly garden, part of a family tree wondering how we got here, and who we are meant to be. "*I AM*" is a mere fractal of a beautiful, but fragmented whole, being drawn towards a deep-seated need to evolve, and listen to the elemental depths of the soul.

LOCATION: AT THE BASE OF THE SPINE

COLOUR: RED

ELEMENT: EARTH

SOUND VIBRATION: LAM

HERTZ FREQUENCY: 396 HZ

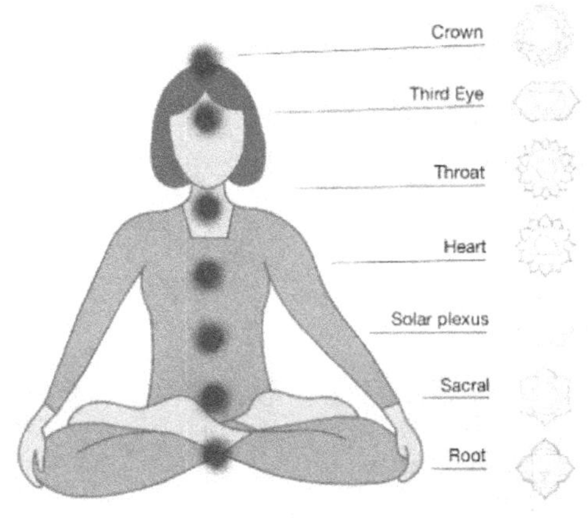

Sonya Bhalla

Global Garden

There is plenty of room
for seeds to take root,
for flowers to bloom
in our shared global garden.
The wild,
the weeds,
the planted seeds,
those transported by birds,
butterflies and bees,
or whisked away
by the summer breeze.

A coloured meadow
flecked with
petalled flares
like firework displays
eliciting stares.
Passing their days
entranced by Sun rays,
breathing the same air.
Nestled among creatures
great and small
all finding their way.

Flowers as free as their pollinators,
as generous as their creators,
as natural as honey hives,
as beautiful as the gift of life.
Together facing the Sun, wind and rain.
Waiting for their cycle to begin again.

Sonya Bhalla

Family Tree

A new tree
rooted in unfamiliar soil.
After many years
of struggle and longing,
finally,
a sense of place
and belonging.

Set in cosy surroundings,
as sturdy as can be
stands the tall wide trunk
of a banyan tree.

Surrounded by trees
of different types.
Some deciduous,
some evergreen.
Some, the tallest
you've ever seen.
Some bearing fruit,
some bearing flowers.
Some fruits so sweet,
but some, too sour.

Taking in the
ebb and flow
of night and day.
Adapting to change
as seasons come and go.

Embracing the Sun's warmth
to the east,
westerly gusty winds
the least.
Reconciling the whirlwind
tensions within.

Assessing nature's ways.
Growing to new heights.
Towering over perennials.
Enduring cold nights.

Deriving strength to weather the storms.
Drawing energy from the Sun,
subsistence from the rain.
Adapting to their environment,
learning to live in rough terrain.

Customs of what went before,
all safe and sound,
winding their way up and out
from roots anchored
deep underground.

Seedlings wanting
to follow their lead.
Seeds scattered far and wide
taking root in another place
when winds are on their side.

With aged circles around their eyes
their judgement more refined.

The view from above
is one of guidance and love.
Tender outstretched branches,
a shade from the Sun,
and a shelter
when the day is done.

Defining Lines

From the moment
a corded lifeline is severed
we're cut loose to choose our endeavours,
but live our lives conforming to lines.

Tied to ancestral and genetic lines.
Searching for other elusive lifelines.

Our fingertips bear
looped lines of identity.
Our palms,
possibly our destiny.

We enter a spherical gridlock
of latitude and longitude;
where outlines of countries
within continents
set boundaries
of beliefs and attitudes.
Illusory boundaries separate us
from everyone else.
A solitude of one,
amongst the multitude
of many.

The underlying stress of fault lines
like burdened vines
coursing through
undulating terrains,
contours of valleys,
mountains, and ridges
like stresses through our veins.

Lines of scaffolds
build bridges
connecting us
beyond these
bordered lines.
Yet we are all
detached
and misaligned.

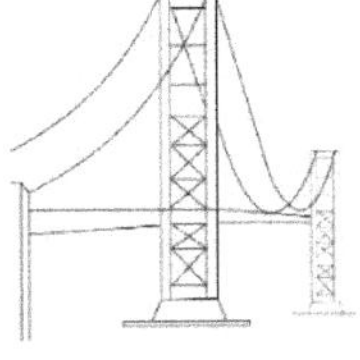

A path.
A chance to map out
our route and find direction.
Signposts lead to a destination,
a new start,
a route connecting
two opposite points
so far apart.

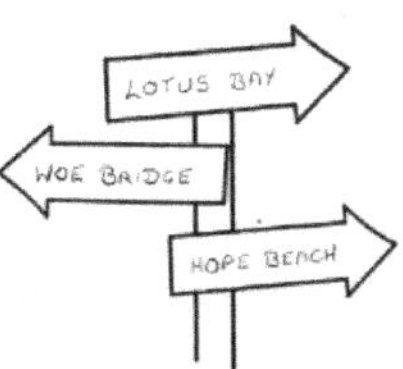

A one-way linear journey
where fate is
bundled into boxed carriages
on fixed train lines.
Tracks carry us to new places,
with new experiences,
new beginnings,
new faces.

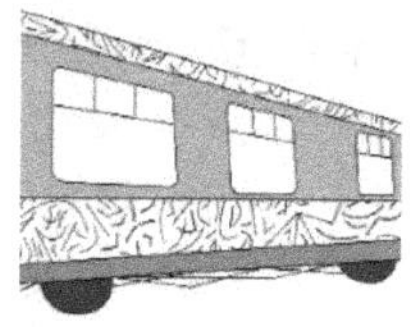

Through the glinting carriage panes,
a glimpse of cities along the way.
Their differing architectural lines
and technical planes
culminating style, design,
structure, and originality.
A testament to
the freedom of creativity.

Pulsating power lines
like dew-laden webs
bring these hubs to life,
as filaments shed the darkness,
like hope in moments of despair.
Interconnecting transmission lines
dissipating a self-centred existence
into one which coexists and cares.

Duties, beliefs, and behaviours
keep us in line.
The efficiency of timetables,
diaries and dials of time
manage our routines.
The courtesy of standing in line
waiting to be seen,
heard, or make our mark
or realise our dreams.

In our youth, learning
the order of geometric lines, arcs,
and the certainty of lineal formulae.
The power of linguistic lettered lines
to read, impart knowledge,
encourage dialogue and connection.
Reading between the lines
when the cursive message yearns
to break free and cross the lines.
Crossing lines we set ourselves
in our mind,
when there is more to find
beyond those lines.

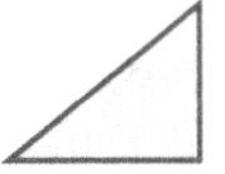

Sonya Bhalla

A string of notes
threading its way through a staff,
as melodies uplift our spirits.

One-liners to make us laugh.

The most famous lines of all time
inspiring us to strive, aspire, survive.

Drawing on stamina, drive,
and grit to reach the finish line.

Conforming to lines
until the heart gives way
and a fluttering pulse
becomes a flat line.

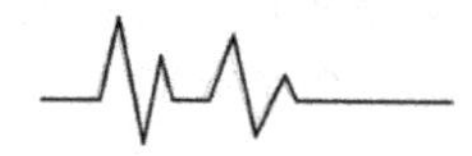

Lines define us, guide us,
lead the way,
navigating us through
our limited timelines,
but allow us to shape each day
in a meaningful way.

Gaia

I stand here absorbing the scene
in a place halfway between
the sky's abundance above
and fluidity of love
below the serene surface
of this beautiful abyss.
Admiring the
stunning sea-swept
golden ridges of sand.
A coastline
where clear azure layers
caress the land.

Radiating a glow
from sun-kissed Sun rays.
My toes melting into a white bay
of pristine grains.
Grains spanning oceanic plains
as Gaia hugged my soul today.

Sonya Bhalla

Anchoring my soles to the floor
as foamy waves roll,
soothe, sway,
and swish around my ankles,
and all woes drift away
with the tide,
and all fears dissipate
like wisps of sea spray.

There's nothing greater
than the soft embrace
of Mother Nature.
Drawing me close to
hear her whisper:
My child, we are the same.
My love for you is true.

Waves of blue
may form and crash
as they reach the land.

But here I stand,
my feet submerged
in comforting sand.

A layer of protection
grounding a connection.

In awe of the sights
and sentient delights
of our transient life.
A tranquil setting
beyond compare.
Feeling the warmth of
the sultry breeze billow my hair.
The smell of salt-laced fresh air.
Hearing the rhythm of waves
as they lap the shore.
Sensing the calm
embalm my core.

The peace,
the calm,
the harmony
of a blissful sanctuary.

Toes melting into a pure white bay
as Gaia hugged my soul today.

The Five Elements

*W*atching the advancing currents of a river
and timeline flow
*A*llowing the fluidity and depths of life
cleanse and set me free
*T*ransparency and purity of soul
strive to reach the sea
*E*xpecting the purpose for which
I joined this lifetime to show
*R*eflective inner soul searching
for who I'm meant to be

*F*lexing to evolve, and connect
within different social masses
*I*dentity, emotions, voices,
and charisma mark a presence
*R*elations and interactions to kindle,
or consume into cinder and ashes
*E*nergy and drive to transform
and ignite individuality and essence

Sonya Bhalla

Appreciating God's gifts: to breathe,
     feel, admire our worldly abilities
Intellect, thoughts, and ideas collude
     to create visions in our mind
Recalling experiences and attuning
     our values and sensibilities

Environmental abundance of flora and fauna,
     its innate beauty to survive and thrive
Awareness of self, our whole being,
     our roots and wondrous sights
Realising our face fronts our outer shell—
     a conduit to live our lives
The fruitful yields of nature nourish,
     heal and nurture our health
Hopes build a grounded base,
     as endeavours grow to new heights

*S*pace fills the gaps and connects

everything in between

*P*erceptions of the unknown, the cosmos,

and elusive divinity

*I*ntuitive presence of phenomena

beyond our realm, beyond compare

*R*eaching for enlightenment, eternal peace,

purity, and unity

*I*ntangible energies of mind, of soul,

of love to share

*T*ransitory existence transcending

unknown dimensions

Wondering about infinite potential, a higher purpose
and how the elements make me, me.

Decoding Nature

Logic is hidden in the wild,
how flowers bloom,
how petals are styled,
in honeycombs,
pinecones and
the smile of a child.

Beyond the random visuals of
our beautiful world,
lies a deeper beauty,
to be unfurled.

In our humble abode,
nature's code
exists in every corner
of Earth's flora and fauna.

Sacred geometry
uncovers nature's
many mysteries.
A language of geometry
with number patterns
of sacred symmetry.

There's a universal order within the chaos,
underlying the creation of us
and our surrounding cosmos.

Sonya Bhalla

You may not see straight lines
in trees, flowers, and vines.
Straight lines
are not how
sacred geometry
is defined.

Numbers, shapes, and forms
surround us everywhere
in music, in crystals,
in whirlwind storms.

Never-ending circles
with no sides.
The infinity of pi.
A unified whole,
a cycle of life
and constant flow
of a toroidal hole.

A sequence of number lines
and mathematical patterns
are life's divine design.

A hidden perfection
to make sense of life.
A spiritual reflection
away from strife.

An intelligent life-sustaining code
woven into intrinsic functions
and different modes;
to harmonise and unify
one and all of us
in a quest to thrive
and survive.

The individual and the collective.
We are all connected.

The Golden Ratio
of 1.618
underpins many shapes.

The series of pi
creates dimensions
of beauty and size,
all pleasing to the eye.

Self-repeating patterns
form fragments of the divine whole.
Made up of clones
which replicate and unfold.

These fractals multiply
in never-ending supply
to form intricate designs.

Like the arrangement of branches in trees.
Like veins coursing through the leaves.

A mathematical sequence
of natural significance.

Fibonacci spirals
can be found
in sunflower crowns,
the Milky Way,
and hurricanes.

Mathematics
is all around,
like fascinating cymatics,
their shapes of sound.

It is believed there was
a point in time where there
was nothing,
then awareness started
moving and expanding.

A circle,
then another,
entwined together.

Enlighten

They multiplied
into the seed of life.
From a flower
came the fruit.
The egg of creation,
a tree of life.

Symbols that stem
from ancient roots.
Relations between points,
angles, lines which correlate,
forming multidimensional shapes.
Platonic solids formed
and continue to transform.

Building block codes
underpin life's blueprint
helping us to understand
imprints of who, what,
and where we are.
DNA helix strands,
atoms, cells, stars,
a drop of water,
a grain of sand.

Principles and spiritual laws
of sacred geometry.
A deeper truth and reality
to a greater cause
uncovering life and nature's
greatest mysteries.

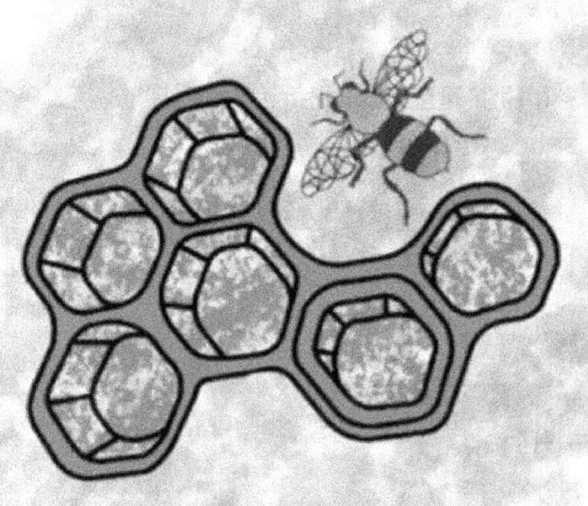

Our Mother Earth

Under a bleak blue halo,
a ripped atmosphere,
a broken Mother Earth.
Her heavy heart
full of pain and fear.

Her abundant layers pillaged
like a peaceful village
left barren, torn, and beaten.

Her ocean plagued by remnants
of man's excess spoils,
toxic waste and crude oils.

Her pretty coastal fringes drowning,
glaciers melting,
her forests burning,
her reefs crumbling.

Many selfish inhabitants
devoid of compassion
and care.
Lost, detached, or
ignorantly unaware.

Sonya Bhalla

Empty vessels on a futile voyage
with faulty compass, no sail,
an uneven keel—bound to fail.

A murky haze hangs in the air,
as pallid rays of sunlight fail to know
why they no longer glow.

Breathless, wheezy, gasping for air,
a tarry smog pollutes her skies.
A corrupt stench stings her eyes.

Oh, how she weeps to flush away
the singed smell of hate
from divisive wars,
and the spilt blood of pawns
to a ruthless cause.

Petals ripped away one by one
by forget-me-not blues and views,
but chances are there's more to lose.

Rotting away like a battered apple,
bruised to its core,
just as environmentalists foresaw.

Some life forms
and natural instinct
on the brink
of becoming extinct.

Like bees swarming
haphazardly
around their hives.
Change is necessary
to survive this ecocide.

Together we can fix what's broken.
Let's create the right conditions to recover.
Let's heal, protect, and love her.

With a mind-shift to embrace truth,
to collaborate as a unified whole,
we can save her body and soul.

Our Mother Earth still has a chance
to flourish and regrow
under a bright blue love imbued halo.

Sand Dunes

Wispy grains swirl, dance and flay
in the wind like chiffon veils.
Blustery currents lift and shape
shifting peaks of sand
like billowy henna-stained locks
below the nape
of a sun-kissed neckline.

Winds imprint their passage of time
across vast plains
like a testament to nature's design,
like a desert sea of sinewy ripples,
like engrained fingertip ridges.

Amongst the mounds and creases
of open palms,
tufts of wild parched sprigs
patiently lie in wait,
hopeful of nature's alms,
to replenish and survive.

Sonya Bhalla

Beautiful
pulsating sand dunes
very much alive
dancing to the tunes
of the sultry breeze.

Quintillion grains
across arid plains
as heavens open
and let loose the rains.

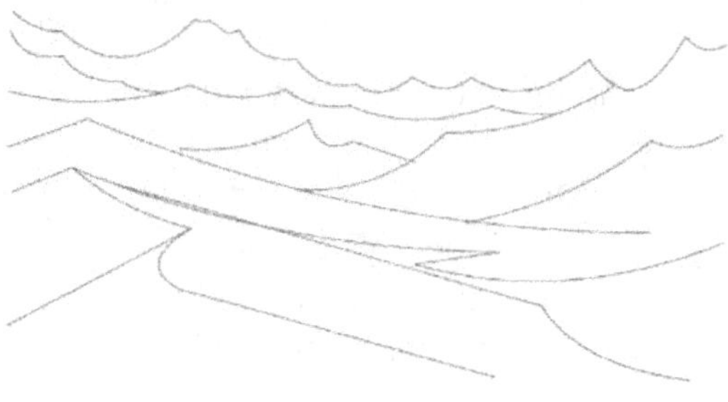

Home Improvements

Step One:
Envision new surroundings.
With great intentions, aim
to declutter and redesign.
'Project Renovation' has begun.

Step Two:
Sift everything you own:
sort and separate into piles.
Discard the old,
embrace the new.

Step Three:
Budget and plan for structural
changes, decor, designs, materials
and labour fees too, before you go
on that shopping spree.

Step Four:
Procure an ensemble of colourful
pots, swatches, and samples.
Assess and dress the potential
spaces from ceiling to floor.

Step Five:
Build in lots of storage.
Safely store sentimental items,
mementos and souvenirs
to keep their memory alive.

Step Six:
For worn and weathered items
which have seen better days,
ready them for a refresh,
upcycle, or DIY fix.

Step Seven:
Shift, rearrange and
try different combinations
around focal features to
create a little piece of heaven.

Step Eight:
For finishing touches, accessorise
and personalise with pots, pictures
and pretty pieces. Keep scented candles
ready for those special dinner dates.

Step Nine:
After a few last tweaks,
stand back to take a view.
Admire the new look.
It's turned out just fine.

Step Ten:
Inhabit comfortable home
filled with love and laughter.
Maintain the ambiance and
enjoy your new peaceful Zen.

Life Audit – A Checklist

<u>Profit & Loss Account</u>
It's that time of year again
to appreciate those gains,
and alleviate
those losses.
A time to reflect
as another year end
review
draws near.

<u>Balance Sheet</u>
In addition,
it's a chance
to chart a future
and plan to nurture
a better life
and vision.

- ✓ It's time to turn over a new belief,
  to evolve and grow.
- ✓ Not operate day to day
  and just go with the flow.
- ✓ So, take stock of all tangible and intangible
  aspects of your life.
- ✓ Prepare a detailed account
  of what brings you joy or strife.

- ✓ Itemise the material, physical,
  familial, and recreational.
- ✓ Also include the mental, spiritual,
  social, and habitual.
- ✓ Analyse the positives
  and the negatives within each.
- ✓ Reconcile the wants, needs,
  and desires to reach.
- ✓ Manage money mindfully
  to ensure a lean bill for wealth.
- ✓ Accumulate compound interest
  for longevity and future health.
- ✓ To avoid debt, live within
  the means of your financial bands.
- ✓ Deduct all the bad excesses
  which devalue your brand.
- ✓ More importantly, enjoy
  great rates of return by just having fun.
- ✓ Spend time following your passions
  or just relaxing in the Sun.
- ✓ Secure friendship bonds
  which lift your spirits when feeling down.
- ✓ Invest time for inner healing,
  well-being, and the power of sound.

✓ Expend energy on gains
which can realise your full potential.
✓ Don't waste it on petty issues
which are inconsequential.
✓ Problems, and negative behaviours are
liabilities we need to decrease.
✓ Compassion costs nothing but generates
harmony and peace.
✓ Grudges, inflated egos, and deceit are taxing
deficits to eliminate.
✓ A safe, loving, comfortable fun-filled fixed
abode is yours to create.
✓ Self-assess every aspect of you.
✓ Give credit where it's credibly due.
✓ Procure a true and fair view
of your inner and outer self.
✓ Review what it means to be
a conscious being itself.
✓ Think in terms of abundance,
gratitude, energy, and auric fields.
✓ Venture into new relations
or collaborations to bring insightful yields.
✓ Invest in self-development
and capitalise on all your qualities.

✓ Acquire skills, review books,
  gain knowledge to maximise abilities.
✓ Don't give up, and don't default
  on precious responsibilities.
✓ Journal an account of daily tasks, feelings,
  reflections, and aspirations.
✓ Partnering can be mutually beneficial
  to share inspirations.
✓ Make allowances for errors in judgement
  and make corrections.
✓ Be accountable for your actions
  and adjust reactions.
✓ Maturity of mind is built
  by nurturing it with love and solitude.
✓ Increase reserves of gratitude
  and vibes of positive attitude.
✓ Find happiness in activities
  with a high level of interest and return.
✓ Save some resilience for growing concerns.
✓ Apportion reasonable time for commitments.
✓ An overflow of debt and material excesses
  is not fulfilment.

- ✓ Operate at full capacity,
  break even on demand and supply.
- ✓ Check the rules and know how to comply.
- ✓ Count all your blessings, no matter how small,
  when life is tough.
- ✓ Know your worth is priceless,
  and you are enough.
- ✓ Live by standards and statements that add
  value to your soul.
- ✓ Invest in your vision for a fulfilling future
  and a meaningful role.
- ✓ Respect your limits to mitigate losses
  and insecurities.
- ✓ We are all work in progress
  with an element of perpetuity.
- ✓ Be appreciative of the abundant landscape
  of our world's beauty.
- ✓ Overall, plan an enriched life
  with a surplus of goodwill.
- ✓ Find a purpose that is profitable
  and yours to fulfil.

CHAKRA TWO

The Sacral Chakra

*"To be creative means to be in love with life.
You can be creative only if you love life enough
that you want to enhance its beauty,
you want to bring a little more music to it,
a little more poetry to it,
a little more dance to it."*

Osho

The Sacral Chakra

The Sacral Chakra (known as *Svadhisthana*) is connected to our pleasure centres, emotions, wellbeing, passion, and abundance. It also represents the cycles of birth, death and rebirth.

The mantra is *"I feel …"* and is all about how we feel about ourselves, others, and life. It's connected to our ability to perceive the outer world as well as connect to our inner world, and gives rise to our thoughts, behaviours and how we act on them. It also covers our creative expressions.

When balanced we can express our emotions in a healthy way, be creative, be open to change, be happy and experience an overall enjoyment of life.

In this chapter, *"I FEEL"* draws similarities between our cosmic life experience and an embryo, that the birth and death cycle may not be the end, that we are love and light beings whose purpose is to transcend. It also FEELs deeply … the grief, the anger, the hurtful remarks from mistaken perceptions and misunderstood intentions. But it also FEELs and believes hope, happiness and harmony is ours to find if we tap into a joyous heart and creative mind.

LOCATION: SACRUM

COLOUR: ORANGE

ELEMENT: WATER

SOUND VIBRATION: VAM

HERTZ FREQUENCY: 417 HZ

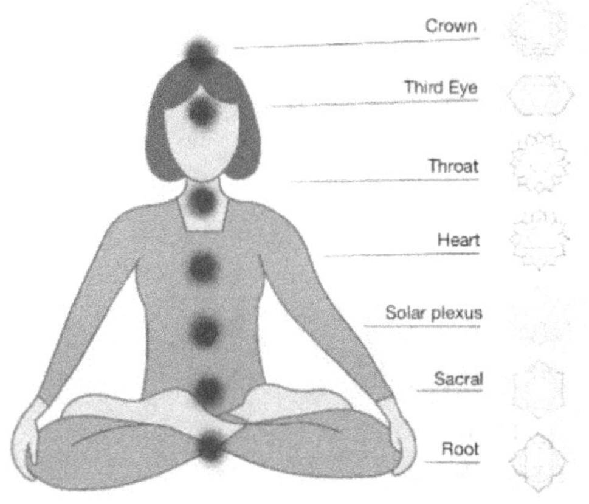

Sonya Bhalla

Embryonic Universe

In a bubble deep within,
is where it all begins.
Floating in an abyss, waiting …
waiting with growing anticipation
of something stirring.

You would think all is quiet
in my little home,
that I am distant,
a stranger
and all alone.
I assure you
my world is warm,
safe, and cosy,
and my neighbour
is active,
noisy and nosey.

The all-pervading
constant beating of a drum.
What a rhythmic companion
of comfort it's become.
Another undulating tone,
never leaving my side.
A canorous world
in which I gladly reside.

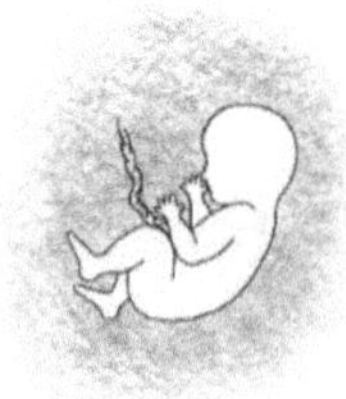

There was a time when
I had lots of space to stretch and swim.
Now only to curl up like a ball,
while the walls are closing in.
My boundaries make me
inwardly focus on me.
Everything else is unknown,
or not meant to be seen.

There are times of upset
and many waves of calm.
A fair balance must be had,
to keep me from harm.
I share in the highs and lows,
but just go with the flow.
However, I am happy where I am,
for it's all that I know.

I experience the bitter,
the sweet and the sour.
Am dismissive to the passing of time
and every hour.
Outsiders try to interfere with my space.
Interactions I sometimes resist,
other times embrace.

Sonya Bhalla

I dream in my moments of sleep,
as dormant visions run deep.
When awake, I am busy
and use all I've been gifted,
to learn, reach out,
discover things I never knew existed.

I am ordinary, yet special
with all my hidden qualities.
Do not underestimate my unlocked abilities
as I wait, ponder, listen,
and discover my surroundings
and lay the path down with new groundings.

There's a presence I sense is there
to love, protect, and really care.
It is truly wonderful and magical,
and the gift I bear is radical.

As with all treasures like me,
unlocking my potential is the key.
For now, I am out of sight,
but I'm destined to shed the dark
and embrace the light.

Sonya Bhalla

Winter Solstice

Darkness descends earlier than expected.
A day cut short by the winter solstice.
I stand here in the cold, dark
stillness of the night,
listening to the onslaught of
unrelenting whispering winds.
Probing. Tormenting.
He's gone.
He's dead.

An inner voice screams back:
It's not true.
It's a bad dream.

A blanket of snow
smothers familial planes.
An interlocking path
no longer visible,
no longer leading the way.

Open palms capture snowflakes
like last words
falling from the heavens.
Mulling over last events.
Still in doubt,
my conscience questioning
as I reminisce.
Did it really happen?
Is he really dead?

The gusts of glacial winds continue.
Why? keeps reverberating in my head.
A maelstrom of emotions
churn and augment inside
like the chills of a fever
rippling through me.
The trauma,
the misery,
the constant heartache.

As the bonfire flames
flicker with rage
against the brazen chills,
fistfuls of anger
fuel resentment,
fuel blame
at life, the world,
the powers that be.

Were we oblivious
to the weather warnings?
Could it have been averted?
Should I believe in destiny?
Is it fate?
Clearly, life is not what it seems.

Sonya Bhalla

I'm now a quivering wreck
as icy temps
permeate every layer
of my being.
Woolly layers have done nothing
to protect me from the biting chill.

I've stayed out in the cold too long.
My extremities painfully
nipped by the frost.
Like the calm
after a whirlwind storm,
the numbness
the emptiness
sets in.
Entrenched in a trance-like state,
yet my mind still whirs.

With salt and grit in hand,
others attempt to dissolve the black ice.
But it feels like
no one can really understand
the intense feelings of devastation,
the heart-wrenching pain
and the permanent void left behind.

A sudden deluge descends from above.
Frozen fractal tears merge with mine,
stinging my eyes.
I cannot hold back the hurt
that streams down my face
as the unwanted realisation
and truth sets in— *he has gone.*

Mounds of snow are pushed aside.
A hollowed-out driveway
gives way to an impetus
to complete a journey.
Nevertheless, desperately wishing to
retreat inwards and hibernate
to survive this harsh winter's night.

The crunch of snow underfoot
reveals indentations on my soul.
One thing is for sure:
life will never be the same.
The fragility of life,
and theories so vexed
heavily weighing
me down.

Sonya Bhalla

Eventually the snow thaws.
Like the rise and fall
of the setting Sun,
I finally come to terms
with the fact
he is never coming back.
Like the death of days gone by.
I accept the inevitable will happen.
Another day will die.

However, love closes my eyes
and keeps hold of
everything beautiful about that day
before it was enveloped by night.
A hope that dawn will break
somewhere else for him
and another day is in sight.

Sandstorms

Red rage plumes
can only blind you
and blur the skyline
if you let them
consume you.

It's okay
to feel the storm
in a fleeting way
without letting it
blur what's good
about your day.

Sonya Bhalla

Gabber Napper

As dusk descends,
a collusive colloquy
crescendos.
Amidst the clink
of cradled bulbs,
nachos,
free-flowing red vino
and jeering banter—
something is looming.

Alluring, yet
unassuming,
she waits,
and fixates
on her target.

Mozzies
disguised as
firepit embers
waft like
smouldering jibes,
intending to
scold and spoil
the party vibes.

A piercing stab
in the dark,
way off
the mark,
but loaded
all the same.

A lame attempt
to swat it away.
But, leaving the social
with a feeling
of malaise.

Later that night,
dragged from
the depths of slumber,
not by the sound
of thunder, but
an uncontrollable urge
to score through
the raging mound
to purge away
the irritation.

Unaware of when
the inconspicuous
beast took hold,
gnawing
at those inner layers.
How it swells and nags
to be relieved.
A fleeting wish
to slay and hate her.

Why are some immune,
while others suffer
potent reactions?
What elements repel,
or attracts them?

Is it the sweetness
or energy they emit?
Let's admit,
if we delve into
the crux of the
matter,
it's bloody goodness
they cannot make
for themselves.

Using balms and barriers
to heal and aid.
Those fleeting banes
of discomfort soon fade.

In the end
pledging to be a fighter
and
donning strong
citrus notes
to ward off
those pesky blighters.

Sonya Bhalla

Misunderstanding

A few words is all it takes,
to break
the strongest of bonds;
leading to misunderstanding
and heartache.

Differences in opinion
causing frustrations.
Or assumptions
or allegations
to shatter
all expectations.

Adverse actions, or
resented inactions,
invoking unexpected
reactions.

A different version of events,
or perceptions,
creating misconceptions
to steer you
in opposite directions.

Failing to clarify,
or things left unsaid.
Sometimes out of choice,
nerves,
or even dread.
With good intentions,
but instilling
ill feeling instead.

A tie, once so strong,
and now,
seeing them after so long
questioning where
it all went wrong.

Allowing so much distance
and time to drift
before recalling
what actually
caused the rift.
Recalling the pain,
feeling so miffed.

Acquaintances
with many a role.
Forgoing the ones
with toxic souls.
Embracing those
who make you
whole.

Later,
on closer inspection,
after deep reflection,
considering
a hope
for reconciliation.

Realising every coin has two sides.
Possible reasons:
perhaps someone's pride.
Not putting misgivings aside.

Accepting our individual experiences
inherently create differences.
Not to be tainted with inferences.

Learning that communication is key.
Explaining so the other can see,
how it was received,
or not intended to be.

Constructively listening to each other
to tackle the issue together,
and not tackle one another.

Having always had a place in your heart.
Wishing, deep down,
you had never fallen apart.
Deciding to forgive and forget,
as it's never too late to make a new start.

Sonya Bhalla

Snowdrops

In the darkest woodland depths
after harsh winter nights,
a hopeful display of snowdrops
splay their white light.

Appearing in full bloom,
casting away
shadows of gloom,
with a will to survive
and thrive despite
snow, rain and
damp terrain.

Rows of droopy streetlamps
laden with cold dew
usher in the hope
to start the cycle anew;
for spring is on its way
to season away
the winter blues
and brighten up our days.

Happiness

Always being sought after,
but never leaving our side.
Having the power to initiate,
but assuming it's been denied.
Postponed to the next goal,
or waiting for perfection.
Not quite as anticipated—
it's a matter of perception.

Always a want or desire,
in our sights, in our minds.
Clearly in front of our eyes
but choosing to be blind.
Always wanting more,
but never satisfied.
Focusing on the negatives.
Instead, choose the bright side.

Thought to be in the future,
but it exists in our daily lives.
If only we could be content,
but despondency is rife.
Often reliant on people's opinions,
when inner peace can set us free.
Felt to be stifled by life's events,
but only if we allow it to be.

Sought from power or financial gain,
but we can count our blessings instead.
Fulfilled by fame, success, or status,
when really fulfilment is opinion led.
Believed to be found in outward beauty,
but seek within and you shall find.
Expected to be found in our material world,
when really it's our state of mind.

Sonya Bhalla

The Universal Language of Laughter

Cue in the laughter.
A boundless, innate
social nexus
of unifying traits.

Giggles and gurgles.
Cute exchanges.
Babbling babes
delighting all ages.

Joyous chuckles.
A splay of tubby toes.
Tummy tickle time
banishing all woes.

Throw-back guffaws.
Enthralling recollections.
Yesteryear chums,
reuniting connections.

Hearty humour.
Doubled up literal lines.
Penny-drop chortle.
Wordplay refined.

A jiggling bod.
A splutter of fits and bursts.
Clumsy mishaps.
Keeling over; oh, it hurts.

Sheer wonder and awe.
Resounding rapturous claps.
Talented displays
no longer untapped.

A throaty titter
diffusing the awkward void.
A jestful remark
intending to annoy.

Sonya Bhalla

Squinting teary eyes.
Uncontainable bellows.
Startling fun pranks
on unwitting fellows.

Hands held high.
Shrieks of sheer excitement.
Thrilling rides
just for entertainment.

Good times, good vibes.
A bit of banter and goss.
Light-hearted moments
away from the boss.

A jaw drop cackle.
Satire, impressions.
Comical spins on life
dissipating tensions.

Blushing rose gold.
Secretly self-amused.
Jittery nerves of an
incredulous move.

Fingertips hiding lips.
Filtered reflexes.
Bemused coy glances.
Battle of the sexes.

Transmissible delight.
A different global contagion.
Spreading peace and joy
across every nation.

Laughter in all forms
one language, one notion.
Unlimited interactions
of shared emotions.

Creative Energy

Let imagination drift and form
     like shape-shifting clouds.
Let musicians tap and try out
     new beats and sounds.

May singers make us swoon
     in awe to their majestic voices.
May tailors sew and weave
     us fashionable choices.

Let dancers clap, swirl,
     and twirl to the flamenco.
Let artisans create pretty trinkets
     and mementos.

May painters' brushstrokes fill blank walls
     with pieces of art.
May authors' imaginations tell stories
     that touch our heart.

May magicians enthral us
        with their amazing illusions.
May chefs entice our taste buds
        with their culinary fusions.

Let lyrics and notes
        dance across the pages.
Let characters and scripts
        play out on stages.

May poets' wise words lift spirits and heal souls.
May all art forms enrich our lives and make us whole.

CHAKRA THREE

The Solar Plexus Chakra

"You find peace
not by rearranging the circumstances of your life,
but by realizing who you are at the deepest level."

Eckhart Tolle

The Solar Plexus Chakra

The Solar Plexus Chakra (known as *Manipura*) is all about strength, ego, personal self-empowerment, self-esteem and self-confidence.

The mantra is "*I do* ..." and connects to our sense of purpose and sense of self through our internal belief systems.

It is the source of our identity, our will and determination. When balanced it allows us to control our lives, have direction and make decisions with clarity and confidence.

In this chapter, "*I DO*" reviews our quilted patterns, delves into the beauty of our inner landscape to self-reflect, discover purpose, and learn lessons to change our ways. *I DO* wonders how to navigate our mystic mind maze and ponders over how pieces of us slot into our puzzling social scenes.

LOCATION: ABOVE THE NAVEL

COLOUR: YELLOW

ELEMENT: FIRE

SOUND VIBRATION: RAM

HERTZ FREQUENCY: 528 HZ

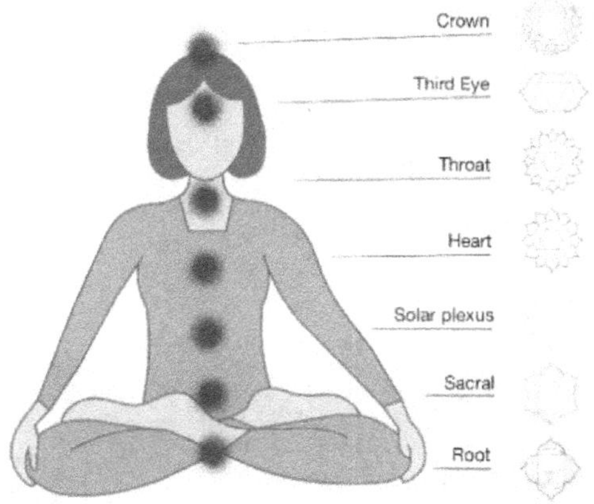

Sonya Bhalla

Patchwork Quilt

Between the seams
are patches of me.
Patches of dreams,
and memories.

Following a theme.
A patterned rubric
made from reams
and reams
of colourful fabric.

Some preloved
sentimental clothing
saved for sewing,
repurposed to make
a lineal keepsake.

Some special motifs,
some swatches of
values and beliefs.

All shaped into squares,
triangles or a mix.
Arranged in pairs
and tacked to fix.

Different pieces
stitched together
to compliment
one another.

Arranged to fashion
a masterpiece.
Vivid patterns
of visions, passions
and inner peace.

A thread of time weaves
its way through the pieces.
An intuitive iron leads
to smooth out the creases.

Between layers of nature
and nurture
a comforter full
of future promise,
some endeavours
to further with fervour.

Cushioned by soft plumes
and a lining of love,
strength and support.
A tailor-made heirloom.

A resilient edge
to frame its final form.
A patchwork quilt
full of warmth.

Beyond the seams
a new purpose,
renewed hopes,
a spread of dreams,
and future memories.

Mirror Lake

A glistening lake reflects and amplifies its surrounding
beauty of clear skies, snow-capped mountains, and
forested pines.

Peering in to find a pretty mirror image,
but in its depths an unsettled visage,
searching for clarity, mindful healing,
and a sense of well-being.

Clear skies: to disperse cloudy thoughts.
A tranquil setting: to unwind and instil peace.
Still waters: remind us to calm the mind and just be.
Its mirrored effect: is time to self-reflect.
Outer beauty: is our cue to resonate beauty inwards too.
Abundant surroundings: need protecting.
Both images: are to be embraced with gratitude.
All are prompts to change our attitude.

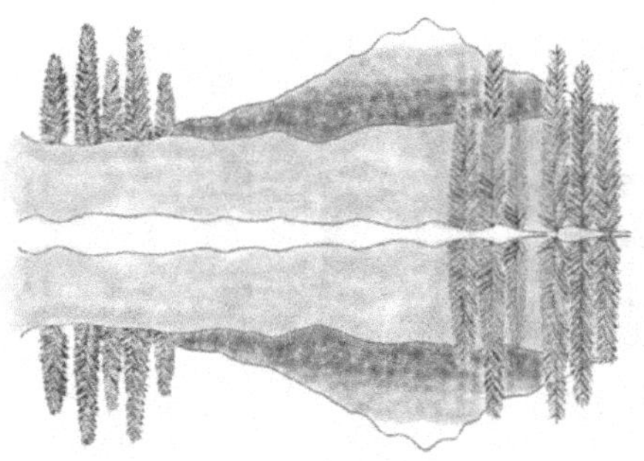

Puzzle Piece

Predestined pieces in disarray,
scattered all over.
Needing help to find their way.
Pieces all different,
some unique,
some bearing similarities
and some disparities.

Each one seeks
a place and a purpose,
longing to fit in.
It's a brain game of detail,
pause, and focus.
An exercise of patience,
persistence,
and making connections.

Eyes transfixed
over shards of an image.
A motley assemble of misfits.
A mind-boggling mix
to be sorted into piles.

Pieces playing an important part.
Contemplating where to start.

Four pivotal corners.
A framed edge to fill a hole.
Interlocking tiles
unlocking spatial roles.
With vision in sight,
an attentive eye locates
the required piece which fits.
Scanning for curvy slates
which possess colours,
markings and shapes
that correlate.

Curves winding up and down,
slotting together one by one
forming a link to the chain,
striving for completion
as mindful contemplation
and adept fingers gain
momentum
again and again.

Pieces forming
parts of a bigger picture.
Like an aperture
opening to expose
a pose or
capture an image.
Finding a visage -
fragments of a sunlit skyline,
windows, a tower block,
of wayward faces
appearing through the cracks
as each piece is aligned.

Clusters coming together
to form one whole.
An image of a bustling city,
its people
emerge from the folds
of the chaos
as it nears its goal.

A mix of oddities,
inconspicuous,
plain,
but requisite
to fit in
lie in wait,
ready to fill the gaps
and fulfil their fate.

The last tile
takes pride of place as it
slots into the final space,
completing a
preconditioned
mosaic.

A satisfactory resolution.
A completed jigsaw
displayed behind a glass pane.
Or, just undone,
only to be put together again.

Life's Purpose

What is life's purpose?
Is it to navigate the journey of life
through a pre-set pathway of barriers,
in a quest to be happier?

Barriers hedged to lead us in certain ways,
like a labyrinth or maze?

Our physical self
through one.
Our conscious self
another one.

A maze
of multiple paths,
where doorways
lead to a destination,
to reach the other end.
A maze of twists, turns,
confusing bends,
facing dead-ends,
or rejection
encouraging
a change in direction.
Making decisions,
feeling lost.
Testing our resilience -
sometimes
at great cost.

Or, is life a path of
opportunities to
grow with the flow,
directing life
like a belief in fate?
Or to backtrack,
learn and know
there is
an ultimate goal?

A labyrinth.
Its entry seen as
the beginning,
the end,
and
everything
in between.

A one-way path
to the centre
spiralling inwards
towards
inner peace.
Back to the core.
Wanting more
than what's outside.
A retreat
to the inside.
A return to source
is nothing new.
Soul searching
to find
a different view.

Perhaps
only a bird's eye view
from a platform above
can see the way through.

A maze — a puzzle to solve.

A labyrinth — a chance to evolve.

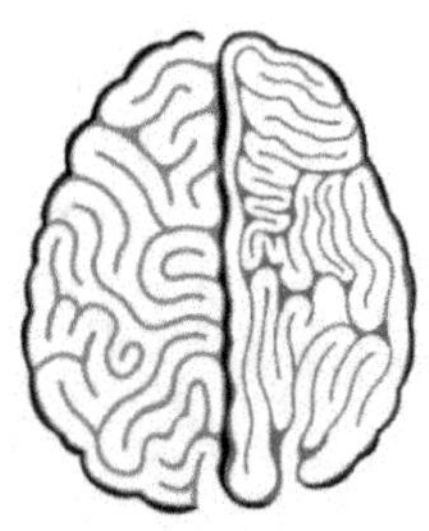

Make-up Routine

A social gathering awaits.
Attentive to my every move,
is my inquisitive child,
perched in my shadow.

Over the years,
a range of attire,
like the many roles acquired,
but today is time for me.

Curves of abundance form my frame.
Choosing outfits, a self-critical task.
Today, opting for elegance and class,
instead of simplicity and comfort.

I cleanse away the disappointments.
Exfoliate away the self-doubt.
Use toner to even out my thoughts
and moisturise to replenish.

Common sense straightens my tresses.
Wispy silver strands denote life's highlights.
Dark circles reveal restless nurturing nights.
Good humour accentuates my fine timelines.

A mirror to reflect and fulfil my dreams.
Cosmetics, perhaps just a facial persona,
but they lift moods and enhance auras.
Taking a moment to be kind to myself.

I review my make-up collection.
Beauty personified in a mosaic of colours.
Brushes applying well-honed basic skills.
Soft sponge blenders to spread some cheer.

A varied palette of attributes.
Feeling the pastels, neutrals, or smoky hues.
Considering new ideas, differing views
as each one completes my presence.

Primer for wit, wisdom, and social acumen.
A layer of independence behind the foundation.
Finding the right combination and shade
to match my tone.
A concealer to hide blemishes, but not my
imperfections.

Highlighter for a unique and special feature.
Contouring bronzer to enhance natural brilliance.
Setting powder for stability, safety, and resilience.
Blusher for modesty and a kind humble heart.

Surveying the face which peers back at me.
Questioning: Am I content with what I see?
Am I everything I want to be?
Over time, learning inner beauty is key.

Eyeshadow to appreciate our beautiful world.
Mascara to refine a positive outlook.
Eyeliner to define and keep focus.
Painted nails for working hands and an active life.

Lip colour to be respectful but assertively articulate.
Gloss for transparency, sincerity, and integrity,
or balm to soothe, heal, and gain clarity.
Lipliner to accentuate and share my smile.

Make-up: just an extension of my essence.
A healthy mindset and authentic attitude
are essential, as is living with gratitude.
Underneath it all: a beautiful conscience.

Accessories to adorn and treasure.
Precious strands hug my neckline.
Studded lobes to listen and understand.
A bracelet depicts life's full circle.

Bands of love, charms and gems I hold dear.
A timepiece to prioritise and manage.
A small clutch to oust the excess baggage.
Sandals to feel safe and well-grounded.

Poised at the dresser,
I consider my reflective image.
No way perfect, but an evolving spirit
learning from life's experiences.

True contentment starts within.
Replenishing rest, hydration, good health
maintains a clear complexion and well-being.
Inner peace radiates a natural glow.

Innocent little eyes look up at me.
Am I content with what she can see?
Is it everything I want her to be?
For her to learn that inner beauty is key.

Confidently beautiful inside and out.
But modestly mindful and self-aware.
Striving to be the best version of myself
with an all-encompassing regime of self-care.

Ambition

Believe everything is possible,
and you're more than capable.

Let these self-motivational
beliefs make you unstoppable.

Life's Lessons

Days become months, then decades.
Before I know it, I'll be old, frail, and grey.
I can't help but pen a note to my younger self
and to my children,
so the gift of life doesn't slip away.

So, I remind them and myself:
Remember life is too precious
to let it pass you by.
Leave your worries and troubles behind.
Don't shoulder problems and inwardly suffer.
Unload your burdens, hold your head high,
and embrace what life has to offer.

Accept that life has its moments of despair.
Admit you have to be a bit tougher.
It's how you overcome your troubles that counts
and what you learn from them is equally paramount.
Appreciate the adage: 'life is not sweet without the
sour'.

Be grateful for what you have,
and don't keep longing for what you don't have.
It is best not to be too materialistic.
It's the simple things we often take for granted.
Always aim to be positive and realistic.

Switch off the autopilot and quieten the mind.
It helps to slow down and take a moment
to value everything around you.
There is so much to admire along the way.
We're too caught up in life's routines to pause and
stare.
Try not to let the routines overtake your life
to the point you just don't care.
Take in all the beauty which surrounds you.

Work hard and enjoy the fruits of your labour
but don't let the fruits cloud your head and heart.
Accept everyone has limitations as well as abilities.
A little patience, consideration, compassion
and understanding go a long way, as does humility.
These are the qualities which will set you apart.

Time slips through our fingers too fast.
Therefore, live each moment as if it's your last,
for only then will you appreciate how fortunate you are
and how much has been taken for granted.
Who knows what the future holds for us
and what we'll reap from the seeds we've planted.

So, feel the Sun on your face.
Feel the wind in your hair.
Treasure those happy and special memories.
Believe the world is a better place.
Listen to the sweet sounds of laughter.
Cherish your loved ones.
And, value your greatest asset, your health.
Most of all, live life to the fullest
and get a better sense of self
and most of all
be proud of who you are
and learn to love yourself.

CHAKRA FOUR

The Heart Chakra

"Self-love has very little to do with how you feel about your outer self. It's about accepting all of yourself."

Tyra Banks

The Heart Chakra

The Heart Chakra (known as *Anahata*) is all about love, acceptance, kindness, compassion, forgiveness and peace.

The mantra is "*I love* …" and is responsible for our ability to give and receive love including self-love, to forgive and understand.

It allows us to trust, be open to new experiences and be accepting of ourselves and others. With this chakra we are able to appreciate the beauty which surrounds us. When balanced we experience peace, joy, contentment, and confidence.

This chapter *"I LOVE"* shares the gift of mothering a child, their playful innocence, and how the essence of true love can enrich our lives. To survive, we must also *LOVE* ourselves enough to know who to trust, how to make ourselves whole and how to avoid those with toxic souls.

LOCATION: MIDDLE OF CHEST

COLOUR: GREEN

ELEMENT: AIR

SOUND VIBRATION: YAM

HERTZ FREQUENCY: 639 HZ

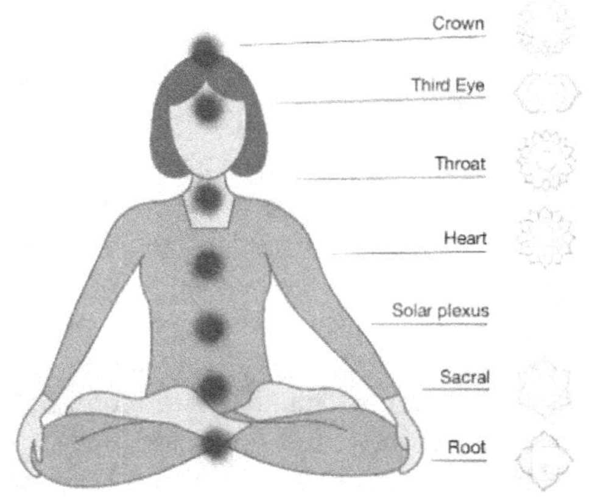

Sonya Bhalla

Motherhood

After nine months of sweet anticipation, a new addition.
Unprepared for the relentless, yet eventful transition.
Child rearing—not as easy as it seems.
A bundle, full of future promise and dreams.
An overwhelming sense of contentment.
A mix of emotions, including love transcendent.
Some apprehension as a first-time mum,
a myriad of challenges to learn and overcome.
A tiny newborn, helpless and dependent for all their needs.
Here come the sleepless nights, endless nappies, and feeds.
Instinctively tuning into their different cries,
you are the most important person in their eyes.
An extraordinary life change that's gladly embraced,
albeit rather daunting, but boldly faced.

Gazing down in awe at their features, so cute and sweet.
Cherishing the chance to nurture, feeling so complete.
Stroking soft tiny hands, admiring a familiar face.
If only time would pass by at a slower pace,
so those quiet moments of bonding may last and never end.
As you promise to always be there, as a mother and a friend.
Capturing, treasuring each precious milestone.
Praising each new effort they've ever shown.
Recording for posterity their first taste, word, and smile.
Watching them develop their personality and style.
Remembering first faltering steps as they totter and stumble.
Rushing to their aid when they take a tearful tumble.
Instinctively navigating the realms of right and wrong.
A role that fits and a maternal pull so strong.

As weeks become months, they soon turn one.
Another exciting chapter has just begun.
They bear a streak of defiance and independence.
With the patter of tiny feet and foolish confidence
they are on the move; there's no stopping them now.
Inquisitive eyes, exploring hands and increasing know-how.
Everything within reach is there for the taking
and clearly meant for breaking.
Touching all those forbidden household things,
with a cheeky smile pulling your heartstrings.
You run after them like their tail,
watching them learn as they try, succeed, and fail.
Getting into mischief, the tricks never end.
But you adore them—even if driven round the bend.

They whinge, cry, and grab your attention every time.
You distract them with toys, food, or nursery rhymes.
Enjoying their sheer laughter when playing peekaboo.
Smiling at their antics as they mirror everything we do.
Dirty clothes, sticky fingers, and a food-smothered face.
Toys and mess strewn all over the place.
Of course, shoes, socks, and hats never stay on.
No longer babies but toddlers—where's all the time gone?
The same old toys can be such a bore.
Never satisfied, always wanting more.
Asleep at last. Time to breathe. Tomorrow is another day
filled with lots of fun and games to play.
Relishing some rest; feeling content.
Reflecting on our day and where the time went.

Their magnetic smiles draw people near.
Baby babble: a language we love to hear.
Conversing as if in meaningful conversation.
Echoes of words no longer needing translation.
Underestimating what's absorbed and what they can do.
'What's this? What's that?'—constantly asked of you.
Intelligent bright eyes always asking '*Why*?'
Attempting to give an appropriate reply.
Appreciating the joys a child brings
as they find happiness in the simplest of things.
Possessing a zest for life and opening our eyes.
Adapting to change; sailing through the lows and highs.
The highlights: a heart-melting smile, precious hug, or kiss.
When apart, an energetic child you cannot help but miss.

As they grow, the demands don't become any less.
The memories formed are of course priceless.
With every stage, await new fears, trials, and joys;
it is so difficult to let go of our little girls and boys.
Always attempting to protect them from harm.
During negative moments, trying to stay calm.
Seeking to steer them in the right direction.
Always ready to give so much care and affection.
Taking pride in their achievements, sharing their pain.
Instilling values you hope they'll maintain.
Willing to make sacrifices and catch them when they fall,
even when they are older and no longer so small.
Whispering silent prayers for their welfare,
due to this invisible bond and love beyond compare.

Like a climbing rose, they grow and develop too fast.
The opportunities awaiting them are vast.
They travel from innocence to experience
full of enthusiasm and persistence.
Clambering as high as they can
they aspire and aim to achieve what they plan.
In their journey with changing face
they collect their building blocks and soon gather pace
acquiring their own experiences along the way.
Hoping they will follow the right path, come what may.
Forming their own views of others, the world, even you!
Inevitably they leave, becoming part of the cycle too.
You remain their scaffold no matter what their quest.
The joys of motherhood—we are truly blessed.

Valentine's Card

Everything I ever wished for, I found in you....

MY LOVE ...
to truly love me with all your heart
that we cannot bear to be apart.
To know you sincerely care and understand.

MY COMPANION ...
to navigate life's journey hand in hand
sharing the ups and downs life has planned.
Promising never to leave each other's side.

MY SOULMATE ....
whom I was destined to find,
that we are one, our souls entwined.
To instinctively know we are meant for each other.

MY FRIEND ....
so we can talk, laugh, and have fun together.
To reach out and turn to one another,
and have a bond which is loyal, genuine, and true.

MY GUIDE ...
so I can depend, follow, and learn from you.
To grow, develop, and improve.
To turn to you for help, support, and advice.

MY CONFIDANTE....
to share everything and never think twice.
Never judging, just ready to listen will suffice
and trust each other, with lots of promises to keep.

MY WELL-WISHER ...
Being content in the knowledge our love runs deep.
Supporting each other when life's uphill climb is steep.
To fulfil our dreams and herald successes in every way.

MY PROTECTOR ...
that you wish for no harm and keep negativity away.
To feel safe in your arms come what may,
and feel secure in the knowledge you will always be
there.

MY PARTNER …
promising a lifelong commitment to love and really care
throughout life and all the events we get to share.
To grow old together and awake each morn with you by
my side.

MY LOVER ….
to belong to you in mind, body, and spirit. In your heart
I gladly reside.
Always on your mind, remembering me with so much
pride.
To be so in love and enveloped by your passion.

MY ONE & ONLY …
to feel that special connection;
and be spoilt by your love and affection.
Knowing I am special and mean so much to you.

My love, may I be everything to you, too.

Phases of the Moon

When hearts are aligned
like the Sun and the Moon,
when the Sun is near
and the Moon is full,
elated tides swell
and swoon,
rolling in and out
to the pull
of invisible reigns
and cyclical boons.

Beware = Be + Aware

Destiny has a way
of revealing a person's
real identity.

Beware of the
selfish users,
narcissist abusers,
thieving scammers,
toxic off-loaders,
and sly freeloaders.

Only embrace those
who are humble, loyal, true,
and genuinely want
the best for you.

Unpleasant Emotions

Let them pass,
learn to grasp
the lesson
and turn uncomfortable
emotional indicators
into positive motivators.

A pressure-cooker hiss of anger
or niggling annoyance
is a signal to hold it in abeyance.
To reflect on why things didn't go to plan.
Understand why it matters to you.
Make peace with yourself and others,
or take a constructive stand.

A slouched deep-seated glum
is dissatisfaction with ourselves
or an outcome.
Find out what went wrong
with a spark of self-compassion
and reignite the passion
that makes you care.
Improve it, fix it, or make it fair.

Squinting eyes,
a frown of disgust or disbelief
is a reminder we're all unique
with different beliefs.
It's a chance to consider
unusual choices,
listen to different voices,
open our mind,
be kind, be wise,
seek facts
with inquisitive eyes,
and check our moral compass
is still intact.

A heavy weight of guilt or regret
is a sign of a healthy conscience,
realising we didn't handle it
in the best possible way.
It's not about blame
or holding onto shame.
You can aim to put things right,
forgive yourself
and change negative behaviours
with the clarity of hindsight.

As fear constricts the air,
the urge to escape the problem
is a trigger for self-care,
or preserve the safety
of our near and dear.
Dare to take steps
to figure out a new path or mindset
away from harm,
impending failure or the unknown.
Face and own your challenges
in a calm, collected way.

Anxious palpitations
and stress-laden beads of sweat.
It's normal to fret
over uncertain events.
It's just a protective prompt
that you care enough
not to succumb
to unwanted outcomes.
Instead latch onto your hope
to turn things around
with a renewed approach
that's safe and sound.

Despair is a cue
to renew your resolve.
So take a break,
take control
and think of new ways
to reach that goal.

Negative emotions.
Let them pass
as you learn to grasp
the lesson
and turn uncomfortable
emotional indicators
into positive motivators.
Learn to live and be
your own content creator.

Resilience

Remember,
mosaics are beautiful pieces of art,
even though
they're made from broken tiles.

Instead of letting broken tiles
become the only fate,
let these pieces shape an image
you wish to create.

Beyond the cracks
is a masterpiece
built and held together
by plaster and glue.

Glue made of
resilience, strength, and resolve.
Let this glue help you evolve,
make you whole again
and create a new you.

Heartbeat

As heartbeats chart our lives
along undulating paths,
let positive values, wisdom,
and resilience fill our valleys.

Let mindful motivations,
selfless actions,
and meaningful connections
climb the mountains.

Let intuitive intervals,
a love of life,
and hopeful dreams
fill the spaces in between.

CHAKRA FIVE

The Throat Chakra

*"To effectively communicate,
we must realise that we are all different in the way we
perceive the world and use this understanding as a
guide to our communication with others."*
Tony Robbins

The Throat Chakra

The Throat Chakra (known as *Vishuddha*) is associated with communication, self-expression and creativity.

The mantra is "*I speak …*" and centres around being able to speak and be heard. It allows us to listen without judgement, speak our truth without fear and communicate authentically and openly.

When this chakra is balanced we can express ourselves freely and creatively.

This chapter "*I SPEAK*" is for speaking your truth, even if it goes against the tide. It hears judgements, different sides, unusual perspectives - all subjective in their quest for justice or newfound knowledge. It hears rhythmic sounds, phonemes and vibrations of energy forming a magic synergy. One of many self-expressive forms of creativity.

LOCATION: BASE OF THE THROAT

COLOUR: BLUE

ELEMENT: ETHER

SOUND VIBRATION: HAM

HERTZ FREQUENCY: 741 HZ

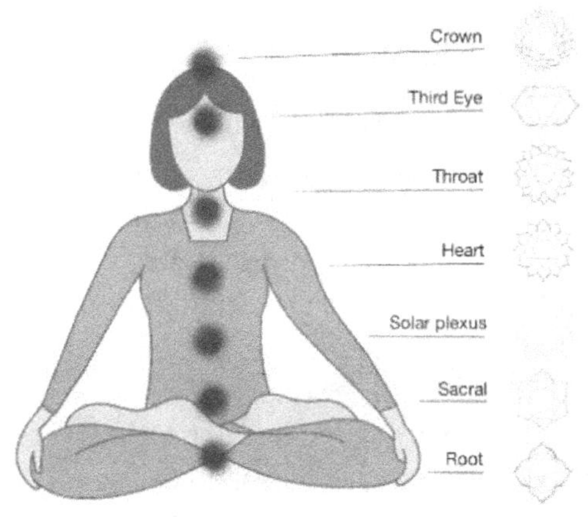

Sonya Bhalla

Balance of Scales

A judge perched high.
A new case to try.
With two sides to every coin.
Another dilemma to intervene and join.
Two adversaries to state their client's case.
Facts and legal issues to consider and embrace,
they aim to tilt the balance of scales
to try: succeed or fail.

The art of persuasion
to get that all-important decision.
A decision maker representing impartiality.
The outcome, a matter of probability.
A system which feels somewhat untoward.
A play of words and a duel of swords
to see if the powerful can be swayed.
Selecting authorities so the system can be played.

A quivering bundle on the witness stand
to tear to shreds rather than understand.
The clever use of evidence
and the fluidity of precedence.
Expecting a search for truth, applying logic and reason.
A notion behind a carefully reasoned decision.
An atmosphere which is formal and tense.
Waiting for punishment, remedy, or recompense.

Is it fair?
Does anyone care
whether the process and outcome are right?
Does anyone appreciate the poor soul's plight?
Sensing an air of nonchalance and arrogance.
What was it that hung in the balance?
Was it money, principles, or integrity?
What about relevance and credibility?

Has justice been done?
Has the right person won?
Knowing decisions could go either way,
that someone will gain, and someone will pay.
A body of laws to govern and protect.
Rules to follow and remedies to correct.
A code of conduct to instil morals and good practice.
Wishing to understand the real meaning of justice.

Perspective

In the distance,
a glimpse of a visage.
The lens of a camera
focuses in
on an image.

Capturing a moment in time
and treasures to last a lifetime.

Different sides develop a point of view,
of what we perceive to be true.

3D into 2D and vice versa is nothing new.
What we believe, or thought we knew,
shapes our worldview.

With different angles to pursue,
creative moves by pioneers
aim to push past
many scientific frontiers
and steadfast barriers.

They crave coherence.

Illusions of depth,
space and appearance
drive decisions
to explore theories
and inspire novel visions.

Through the viewfinder,
is a depth of view
finding new dimensions
of me and you.

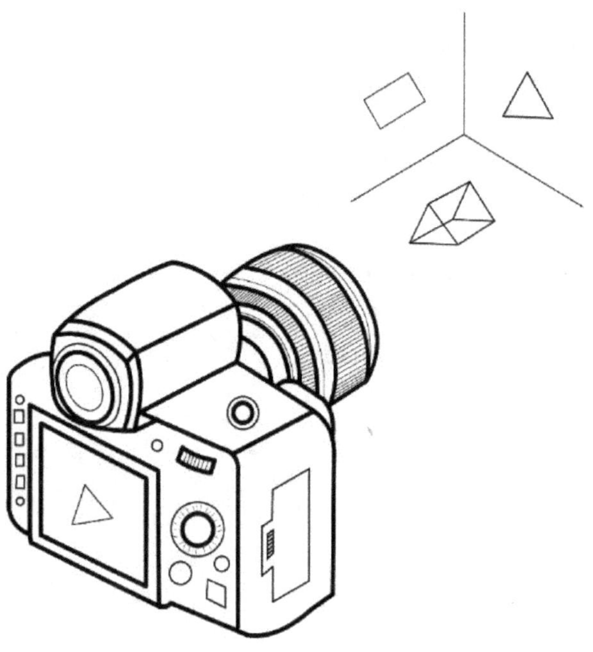

The Sound of Music

Raindrops drum
on a windowpane.

Drum kits crack
in crowded rooms.

Both channel waves
into pleasing tunes.

Resonating moods
like shifting peaks
of desert dunes
and smooth sands.

Some happy, some sad.

Influencing our memories
like imprints
of a babe's hand.

A first dance, a nursery rhyme.

Intangible
forms of song
surpassing time,
beckoned on a whim.

Stored on sims,
vinyls, discs, mp3s,
in our hearts,
brains,
our memories.

Triggering innate impulses
to hum, sing along, and
surf the undulating waves.

DJ mixers, speakers, CD players.
Boombox volume, feel the bass.

Hit play, pause, repeat.

Tap your feet.
Glide and flex
to cycles of a beat
like synchronised
flocks of starlings.

Dancing to hip-hop, salsa,
jazz, tango ...
the list goes on.

A favourite song.
An attractive companion
reeling you in
with hook lines of love,
comfort, and understanding.

For romancing couples
when together and apart.

Or a tonic for afflictions of the heart
like the heady soothing notes found
in a glass of red.

Lyrical sentiments strung
on a piece of thread
like the poetic blend of spicy aromas
swooning off a culinary plate.

A chance to create
a series of verse, chorus—
an eclectic synergy.

Awaiting rhythmic bursts of energy
like a New Year's firework display.

Timbre. Tempo. Tone.
Pitch. Pace.
Intonation.

Often a way of switching off from
daily humdrums.
To submerge into the fluidity
of auditory dimensions.

Headphones.
Concerts.
The heartbeat of a mother.

A multifaceted phenomenon like no other,
connecting, communicating, uplifting souls.

A whole universal orchestra
pulsating through our lives,
making noises.

It's nature's voices
striving
to coexist and survive.

There's harmony between
the fuzzy hum of a bee,
and wheezy wind
rustling the leaves,
weaving its way
through the trees.

Music on stage.
A flutter of notes
on a musician's page
like a string of fairy lights
dancing across the sea.

Rock. Pop. Classics. RnB.

Iconic songs playing
in the background.

Sounds.
Vibrations of energy
connecting everything
in this universe
at different frequencies.

Cosmic mysteries.

Sounds of music.
A tonic for good health.

Its profound ability
to enrich our souls
and sense of self.

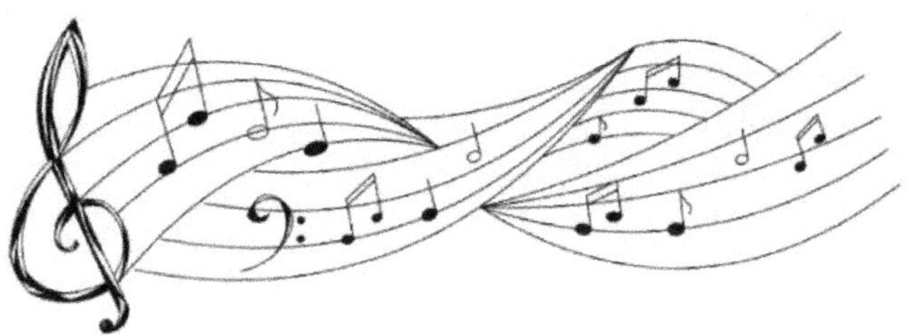

Sonic Tonic

The science of sound.
A profound form
of well-being.
A newfound
way of healing.

Embalmed in a
bath of sound,
I lie on the ground
with outstretched palms,
inviting a deeper calm.

A vibrational song
of singing bowls,
a gong,
some vocal hums,
chimes and drums.

Circling rims.
Sensations of
tingling limbs.
A few chills
as I lie so still.

Floating amongst waves
of notes and octaves.
A meditative symphony
of purposeful frequencies.

Rediscovering Vedic teachings
channelling deeper meanings.
Like mantras of sages
passed through the ages.
A legacy of spiritual codes
harnessing ancient modes
of universal resonance,
a molecular presence
and inner essence
of a different kind
to protect the heart
and awaken the mind.

Adrift in a vibrational world
as occasional chilly waves
swish, swirl, and surge past,
through vast layers of our existence.

A different soundscape.
A soothing escape.
Feeling at ease
with a sense of peace.

Resonating in an alternate reality:
that we are all energy
on a spectrum,
longing for unity
and cosmic synergy.
All attuning to a universal
pulsing signature
of a quantum overture.

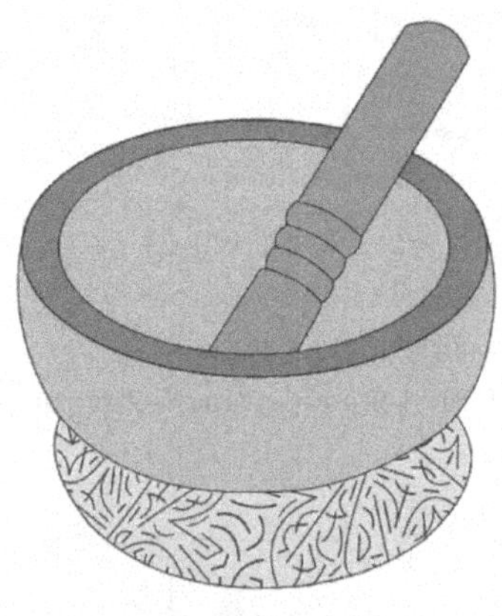

Bubbles

Wandering thoughts
are like floating bubbles.
Let them burst,
or let them be.

Let the light of your thoughts
bounce off their surface,
glisten and reflect back
into colourful creations for all to see.

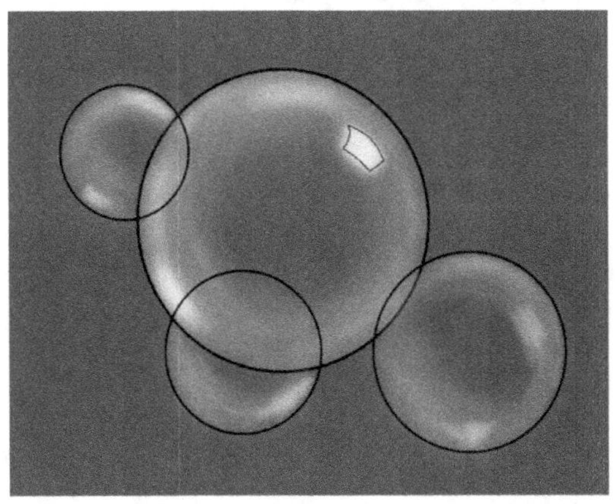

Sonya Bhalla

Tumbling Words

Finding new words is like
spotting the best stones on the
rocky shores of a lake.
Deciding which to leave,
and which ones to take.
Accumulating attractive ones
in a mental container,
and saving them for later.
Placing them in a barrel to tumble.
Filling it up to three-quarter
with grit, rocks, and water
to knock and remove
the edges and move
them into their final form
until they're shiny and smooth.

Bringing out their beautiful
inner colours and tones.
Taking time to make an
appearance as
a semi-precious stone.

Eventually setting aside time
to elevate its purpose.
Using another craft
to create another
beautiful piece of art.
Thoughtfully selecting
perfect ones to repurpose,
arrange on a box, planter pot,
or just display, or collect
and find a use for them
on another inspired day.

Sonya Bhalla

Artistic Visions

Upon the artist's palette
lie clusters.
Misshapen coloured clusters
resembling continental masses
full of character, diversity,
feeling, and meaning.
An inviting blank canvas
expansive as the ocean,
candidly awaiting inspiration
to enrich and flood
its stark demure frame.

A spectrum of colours
merging, blending, diluting into
a mosaic of diverse shades,
tones and hues.
Expressing conditioned features.
Some personify warmth,
peace, and comfort.
Some radiating bright,
refreshing, or calmer tones.

Others depicting the dark,
cold, or mysterious,
danger, passion, or our lifeblood.
Colours accentuated by
the defining contours of black.
The blending softness of white.
A spectrum striving for balance,
harmony, grace and rhythm.

In awe of the creativity,
concepts and ideas
which freely flow
through the artist's wand;
the expressions
they partake on the canvas
and the wonders they encapsulate.
Colours strewn across a space
to meet, co-exist, compliment,
or contrast each other
to form a masterpiece.

Sonya Bhalla

A vision, scene, or portrait
captured by the artist's eye.
Spectacular visions
so time can stand still
and we see nature's
unsurpassed infinite beauty.

Like slender silhouetted
deep-rooted trees
against a backdrop of
a blushing Sun setting sky,
its red globe sinking under the horizon.

Or the overwhelming views
of towering snow-capped mountain peaks
piercing the streaky blanket above,
overlooking forested landscapes and winding rivers,
pure quilted patchwork countrysides,
and skinny roads flanked by a tunnel of trees
dusted with icing sugar on a crisp frosty morning.

As compared to
uneven charcoal grey linear structures
and soaring glinting glass towers
closely packed together forming
the nerve centres of our cities.

Such is the gift to capture
our stunning unspoiled natural settings.

An assortment of materials and
charismatic artistic flare and style,
different hues, shades, and tones
freely flow with no particular outcome in mind;
allowing thoughts to diffuse into the blank pane,
watching it all evolve to create a rogue piece
absorbing all the feelings from within.

Different patterns,
textures, and abstracts
creating new designs,
techniques, and perceptions
displaying characteristics
and feelings frozen in time
known to the creator.
But, left to the beholder
to admire, speculate, discover,
imagine or interpret.

All snapshots of the many
sights there are to see
in our beautiful world,
visions behind our mind's eye.

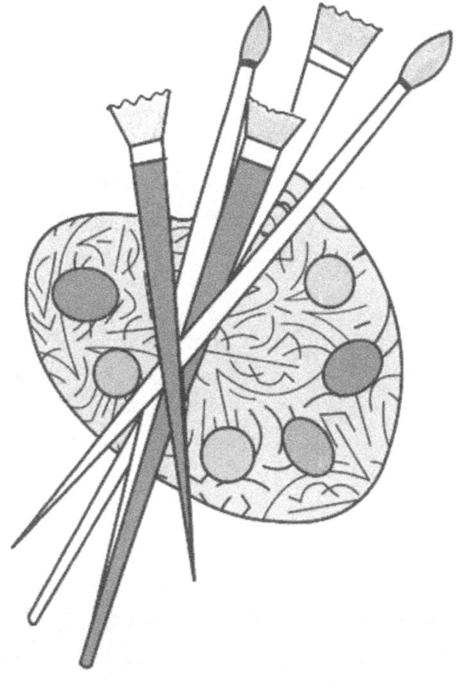

CHAKRA SIX

The Third Eye Chakra

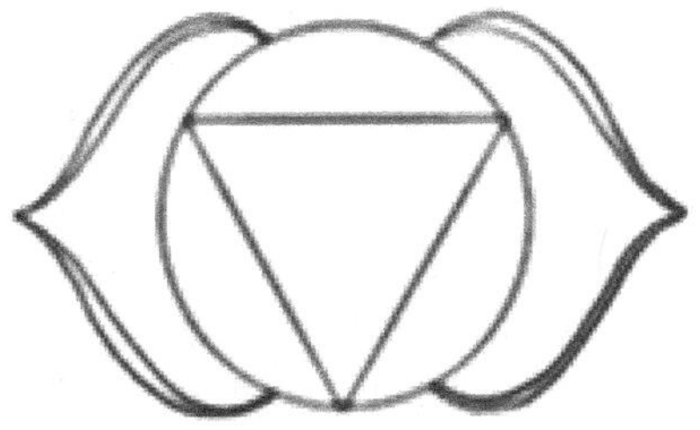

"Who looks outside dreams;
who looks inside awakes."

Carl Jung

The Third Eye Chakra

The Third Eye Chakra (known as *Ajna*) is the centre of intuition, insight and wisdom.

The mantra is *"I see ..."* and is like an inner guidance system, allowing us to think, reason, perceive and make decisions. It is also associated with abilities to see beyond the physical realm and access higher levels of consciousness.

It is seen as the gateway to spiritual awakening and enlightenment. It also allows us to manifest our dreams and desires. When this chakra is balanced we are able to make decisions for the greater good.

In this chapter, *"I SEE"* considers how despondency grows, but seasonal splays of hope come and go. It SEEs reasons to trust our intuitive inner eye when we dream, perceive and believe beyond the tunnel vision of the preconceived. It reveals the wonders of our universe, our mind and how our inner essence can escape and shine.

LOCATION: LOCATED BETWEEN THE EYEBROWS

COLOUR: INDIGO

ELEMENT: LIGHT

SOUND VIBRATION: OM

HERTZ FREQUENCY: 852 HZ

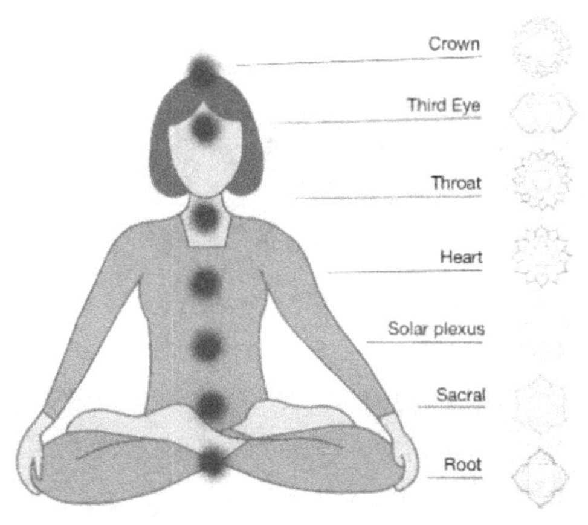

Sonya Bhalla

Spring

When I think of spring
I think of the joys it brings.
Waking to an incredible view
of morning dew,
swathes of daffodils,
snowdrops,
other buds too.
Birds nestled in blossoming trees,
a cool, crisp welcoming breeze.

Yes, there's something special
about the fresh notes of spring.
Birds trill, shrill and sing,
oblivious to what's gone before.
Their outstretched wings soar
the bright clear skies.
Eggs and offspring signify
new life, new hope, new beginnings.
Their nests made of finder-keeper
resourceful winnings.

Scents of freshly mowed grass
and floral hues
are cues
to breathe in fresh air,
listen to nature's muse,
stare at all the beauty
and enjoy these incredible views.

Sonya Bhalla

Dream Catcher

Successive strands
of woolly images,
stories, and messages,
are like
short film reels
weaving their way
through the hoop
of my mind,
feeling so real.

Many flying away like
feathers in the wind—
difficult to pin.

Some captured.
Some interesting.
Some just bizarre.

Sitting up in bed.
Sitting with how it feels.

Beads dangle like impulses
to decipher what they mean.

Threads crisscrossing
unconscious layers
of my ethereal being.

But I shrug them off.
Deciding to let them be.

Dreams:
a woven web
of elusive strands
and
everything in between.

Sonya Bhalla

Instinct

Instinct is a nagging qualm
to take a different direction,
to give in to a calm
intrinsic perception.
Like a child tugging
on your hem to gain
your undivided attention.

Listen.

Embrace her with open arms,
she's telling you to follow your heart,
to feel the vibrations
of your soul.
So, let her guide you
out of that indecisive hole.
Let fate unfold
and fulfil its role.

Kaleidoscope

What do you see
when you look inside
a kaleidoscope?

Perhaps just a toy
with optical illusions,
a tunnel vision
of random items,
a division of patterns.
Or perhaps it invokes
something beyond the scope
of mere objects colliding
and swirling at the end of
a mirrored hollow tube.

I see …
inanimate objects
coming to life,
wild and free,
through clever lines
of symmetry.
Mirrors evoking
a multitude of unique
and complex designs,
as many as infinity.
Reflecting ordinary pieces
into visions of beauty.

Sonya Bhalla

Each time I look inside,
I'm truly mesmerised
and yearn to see
the dazzling colours,
abstract fragments
morphing
time and time again
into yet another
intricate random pattern
with every turn of the dial.
Aiming the lens towards the light
making the view
even more worthwhile.

Sometimes I see
flowers blooming,
stained-glass windows,
dancers swooning,
oriental rugs appear,
glinting chandeliers,
a treasure trove of jewels,
art deco souvenirs,
synchronised swimmers,
flowers reappear,
then disappear.

I also see
thoughts somersaulting
against the rim
of infinite possibilities.
I see a chance to adjust,
turn and reframe
them into opportunities
and worthwhile activities.

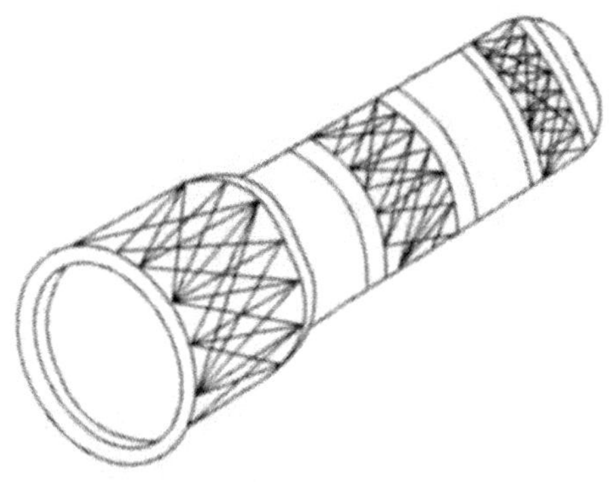

Sonya Bhalla

Conspiracy Theory

Love, love, love
how the universe conspires
to weave its magic,
connecting and inspiring us,
to learn and evolve.

It's as if it can feel
the vibrations of our soul.

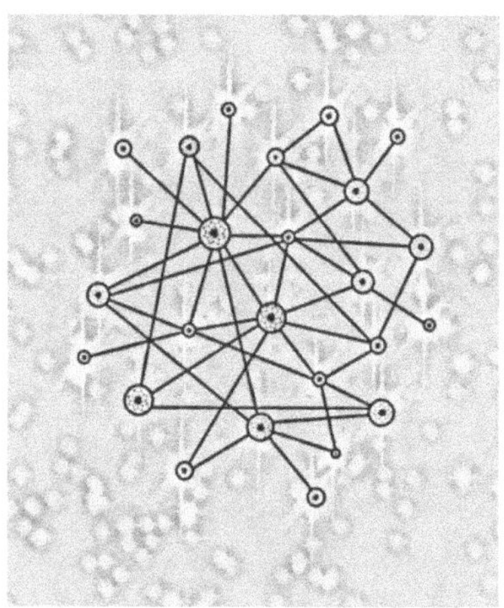

Bindi

Above the brow of the horizon, a centred red Bindi.
A symbolic beauty spot adorned by an Indian lady.

A vibrant globe, a vital solar energy source.
A chakra, a spinning orb, connecting bodily life force.

A blushing pastel sky and sunsetting coastal hues.
A newly married bride wearing a smidgen of sindoor.

Graceful curves sweep the length of the coastline.
An indigo sari drapes across her tanned neckline.

Our sensory fringes melt into sea-swept golden ridges.
Its grainy infinite potential to reveal universal bridges.

India's peninsula parting the expanse of the Indian
Ocean.
A temple led by ancient customs and yogic
contemplations.

In the distance, an untrained yacht owner sails aimlessly
on the high seas.
A vessel of mere physical existence, skimming the
surface of what could be.

The serenity of the sea glistening in the sunlight.
An inner wisdom of consciousness, peace and light.

Peaks and troughs of waves—a constant flow of energy.
A chakra gateway to plexus strands— a unifying synergy.

Delving into the soothing depths of an underwater world to thrive.
An opportunity for spiritual awakening through an intuitive third eye.

Above the brow of the horizon, a centred red Bindi, full of radiance.
A symbolic beauty spot of deep spiritual and cultural significance.

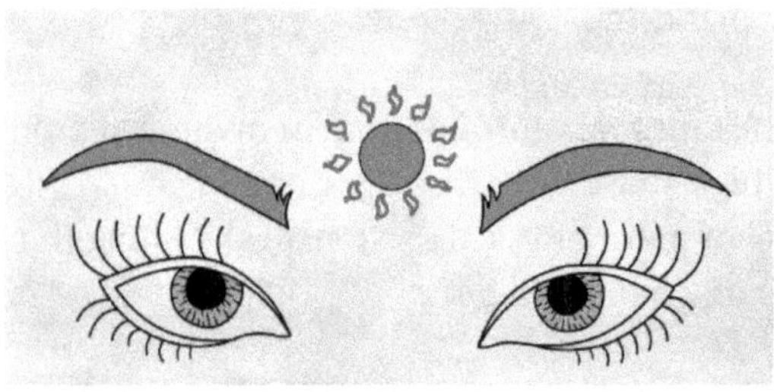

Behind Our Eyes

There's a room with a view of the great outdoors.
But there are reasons to stay indoors.
It's a beautiful home,
calm and airy,
with a comfy chair,
and neutral tones.

As the Sun and Moon rhythm the sky outside,
a pair of sensory windows project
reflections of light, messages and images inside,
and induce waves of calm to sleep at night.

An outward world of physicality
influence our visions,
our wishes,
our perceptions of reality.
Like salty beads shed with broken vows.
Annoyed creases between the brows.
Or, crow feet eyes, a rosy crescent of joy.
Life is full of choices.
Windows and sounds glimpse a feeling,
letting light in
to cast shadows of thought
from floor to ceiling.

Yes, our eyes bear expressions of emotion.
But, a third sees beyond the halt of light
and bears a notion just as bright.
Perceiving things we cannot see.
Another eye, another dimension.
A profound perception
that there is divine synergy
and connection.

A higher bulb of energy,
a gland deeply centred to cast an inner fire
to light a path to Shivalry.

It's time to draw the curtains
and let the light in,
and shine bright from the room within.

Sonya Bhalla

Escape

In the midst
of life's daily grind,
I find solace in the written word,
in words that I've heard.
How they unfurl in my head.
How my scrawls and scribbles
curl across a page,
revealing purpose,
aspiring to be read.

In the midst
of life's daily grind,
I find a whole new world
as I curl up in a reading nook
and submerge into the folds
of a riveting book.
A mysterious plot unfolds;
I'm hooked.
Held captive for ages
in its spellbound pages.

In the midst
of life's daily grind,
I find synergy in song.
Attuned to a vibrant energy
and the urge to sing along.
Adrift in the sea of life.
Making me sway
to rhythmic waves
and soothe away
the wrongs.
Lyrics striking a chord
within my core,
drifting back to shore.

In the midst
of life's daily grind,
I find freedom in art.
An outlet to prise apart
mere existence
and essence of the heart.
Filling a blank canvas
as the mind roams free.
Awash with colours
to feel and see.
Unlocking creativity
and expressions of me.

Sonya Bhalla

In the midst
of life's daily grind,
I find a sense of peace.
A presence of self,
a form of release
from humdrum routines.
Delving into nothing
but my inner solitude
and a place of gratitude.
Emerging feeling renewed,
with a different attitude.

In the midst
of life's daily grind,
I find these forms of expression
are alternate dimensions
to channel emotions,
to escape, rest, heal,
gather thoughts,
transcend,
and feel a sense of self.
Or embalm my soul
with a future zeal.

In the midst
of life's daily grind,
let's take the time
to escape.
Perhaps a divine gift
of a different kind
awaits.
An outlet that's
yours to find,
which will make
your inner essence
unfurl and shine.

CHAKRA SEVEN

The Crown Chakra

"Our biological rhythms are the symphony of the cosmos, music embedded deep within us to which we dance, even when we can't name the tune."
– Deepak Chopra

The Crown Chakra

The Crown Chakra (known as *Sahasrara*) is the highest chakra before the Soul Star, Stellar Gateway, Universal Gateway and the Divine Gateway.

The mantra is *"I know ..."* or *"I understand"* and influences our brain functions, including memory, focus and our intelligence. It is all about spiritual connection, enlightenment, and divine wisdom. It is believed to be the gateway to higher consciousness and a source of all spiritual energy.

It allows us to access our inner intuitive wisdom and think, reason, and imagine. We strive for spiritual growth and strengthen our connection with our soul and spirit. When this chakra is balanced, we have a sense of peace, harmony and a feeling of oneness, or connectedness with the universe.

This chapter *"I KNOW"* uncovers ancient wisdoms and modalities which can enhance our mental faculties, perhaps tap into Akashic memories; holds theories that we are cyclical beings in a realm of healing, and we can spiral a cosmic connection for conscious wellbeing.

LOCATION: TOP OF THE HEAD

COLOUR: VIOLET

ELEMENT: VIBRATIONS

SOUND VIBRATION: OM

HERTZ FREQUENCY: 963 HZ

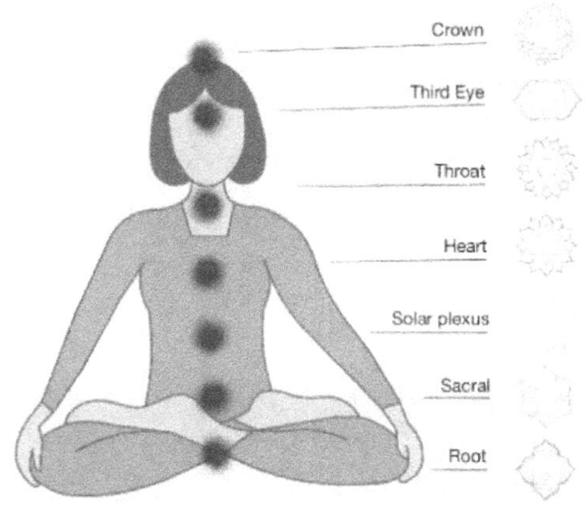

Ancient Art Forms

Yoga and origami.
Art forms of ancient origin.
A practise of balance,
flexibility, and discipline.

An elemental paper square
stretched out
ready to bear
a sequence of moves
following
contemplative rules.
Measured instructions
of dots, dashes, and
symbols signal
creases
in all the right places,
like pieces of a plan.
Lines coming together
until a snowflake's spine
appears at its centre.

Like a yogi on a patch
of grass,
arms by their side,
then
stretched out wide,
legs apart.
Striking a pose:
a five-pointed star.
Slowly bringing palms
together
at the centre of the
heart,
welcoming inner
peace,
a sense of calm,
with a graceful stretch
and release.

A sequence
of manoeuvres.
Prepared creases
in each section.
A repertoire of folds
in different directions.
Embodying
valley folds,
mountain folds,
to set a series of waves
in motion.

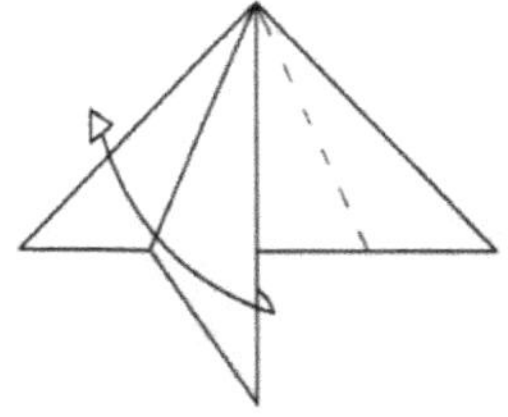

Sonya Bhalla

Concentrating
on the deep inhale,
feeling the rise and
climb of the breath,
then
the gradual descent
on the exhale,
releasing all tension,
as the body glides
into each position.

The mindful bend
and flex of paper,
folding over.
Opened-out corners,
an arrow to turn over,
lines to reverse, squash
and crimps are
aligned into place
as it takes shape
into a paper tree.

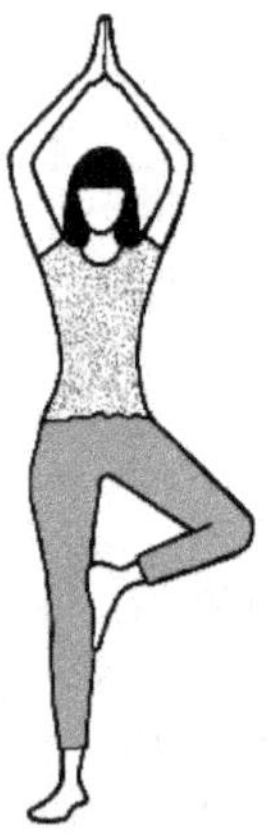

Slowly raising left foot
for sole to meet the knee.
Holding steady
to form a tree.

Mindful movements
evoking moments of calm.
Meditative movements
like a sedative balm.

BREATHE. BELIEVE. BE FREE.

Memories

No amount of money
can buy us happiness.
Our memories,
without a doubt
are priceless.
They are our
greatest assets
and our
most valuable accounts.
So make them count.

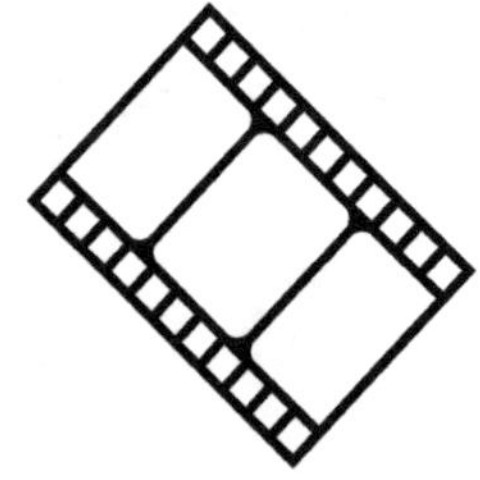

The Water Cycle

Drops of soul in a realm of being.
Where seeing is one form of believing.

An abundant ocean sways and flows in tune
to the wax and wane of a silver Moon.

It's glistening waves dance
under the gaze of a bright sky.

Both, a conscious expanse of life,
with essential minerals to survive and thrive.

Realms of fight and flight,
love and light.

As warmer days
and Sun rays
reach the surface
of the ocean,
drops are chosen
to shed their fluid form.
Setting in motion
a journey
to rise,
to reform,
to transform.

Sonya Bhalla

As essence ascends
to higher plains,
they disappear from view.

Cooler temps ascend too
for a calm, connected plenum
and divine truth.

Dew laden cotton clouds drift
and streak across the blue.

Essence destined to return again
as heavens open to release the rains.
Precipitating back to Earth in different ways.

Liquid life meandering down mountains,
channelling their own pathway.

A downpour moulding
and moving with the flow,
as riverbeds lead the way.

Gathering in streams
to journey to the sea.

Sporadic showers seep
back into layers deep underground
replenishing plants and trees.

Some trickling into crevices,
slipping through tough straits.

A deluge destined to speckle the seas
and ripple across stagnant lakes.

A continuous renewal of energy,
as life goes full circle.

Drops of soul in a
conscious cosmos,
where being
is eternal.

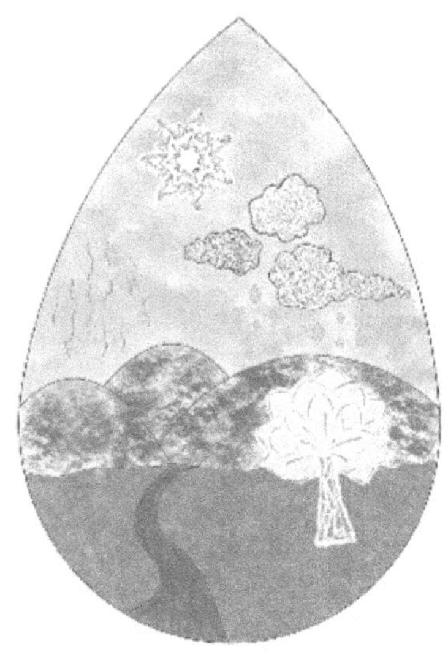

Sonya Bhalla

Lotus

Dormant seeds
await their revival.
Naturally
craving survival.

Sprouting life
out of the deep
depths of a
laden sleep.

Tuber roots
lie awake
counting hours
till daybreak.

Slender stems
reach up high
like kite lines
in the sky.

A closed
weary bud
emerges from
a bed of mud.

Petal layers
tightly hold
onto thoughts,
later to unfold.

Opening to the first
rays of sunlight.
By mid afternoon
retreating for the night.

Cupped awareness
leaving no room
for fleeting thoughts,
as soul starts to bloom.

Beads of water slide
off a waxy coat,
as aquatic leaves
resist and float.

Like letting go of
worldly distractions,
as inner peace
gains attraction.

Unfurling even more
the next day,
shedding murky
waters once again.

A symbol of purity,
unwavering faith.
A sacred presence
of beauty and grace.

A chance to evolve.
Feel tranquillity
in serene waters
and embrace simplicity.

As petals fall away
in sweet surrender,
a crown jewel is
left at its centre.

Emptying its mind
a sense of clarity,
a renewed energy
to tackle adversity.

A flowering consciousness,
mesmerised by the Sun's rays.
A life cycle completed
in a matter of days.

A pathway to transform,
seek truth, ascend
to a pristine existence
and spiritually transcend.

A lotus flower.
Murky waters forsaken
and a chance
for souls to reawaken.

A Soul's Journey

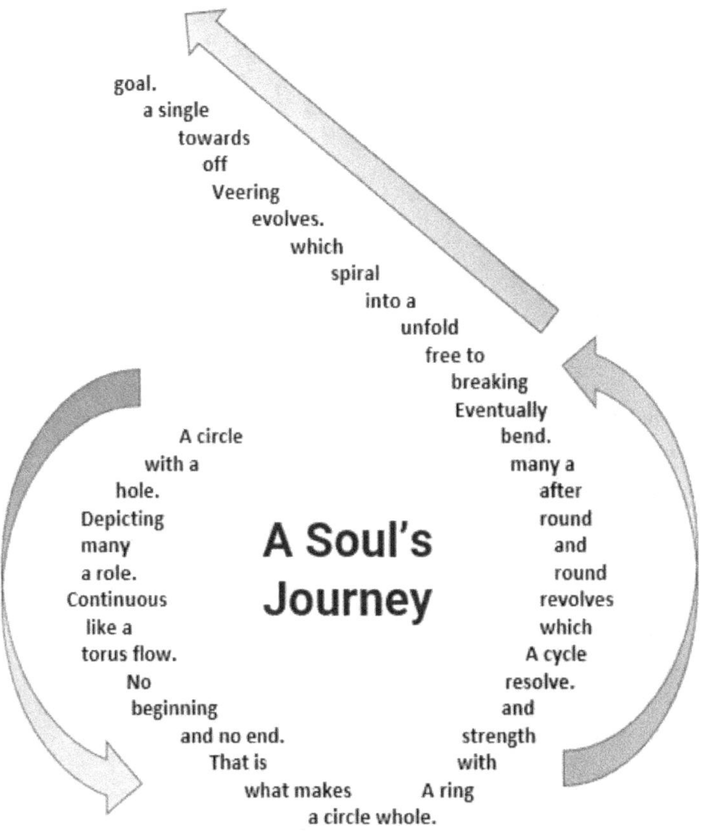

Sonya Bhalla

Stardust & Starlight

The origins of us
came from
cosmic dust.

We are the Sun,
the Moon and Stars
shining bright.

Out of darkness
came light.

It all started
billions of years ago
with stellar implosions,
molecular fusions,
planetary contusions
forming our galaxies today,
vast constellations
and the Milky Way.

Out of a cosmic dawn,
our Sun was born,
Stars were formed.

Debris flung
far and wide,
forming planets
as forces
caused rocks
to collide.

The story of Earth
begun
as gravity shaped our
Earth, Moon and Sun.

So did years of
turbulence and strife.

Out of dying Stars
and icy rocks
came the building blocks
of life.

As evolving elements settled,
atomic seeds of us nestled
until Theia's' rage
hit Earth into a new age.

Bowing to the Sun,
our seasons were spun.
The pull of the Moon
made tides
swell and swoon.

Creating elemental beings
so diverse.
We are descendants
of this Universe.
Part of a spectrum
of waves
flowing to the rhythm
of solar rays.

So, as we gaze
at our amazing
star-studded night sky,
remember you and I
are also starlight
shining bright,
and stardust
of the cosmos
flows within
each of us.

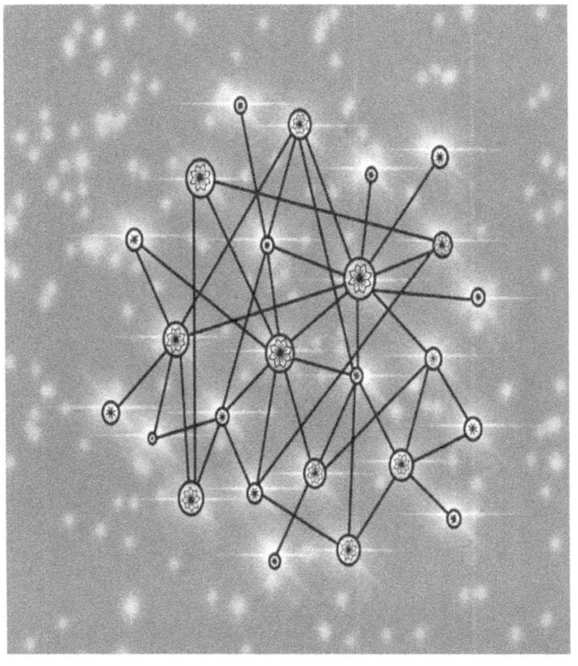

ALL CHAKRAS & BEYOND

*"If you want to find the secrets of the universe,
think in terms of energy, frequency and vibration."*

Nikola Tesla

ALL CHAKRAS
& BEYOND

This chapter which I have summarized as *"I EVOLVE"*, aims to transform, embrace the light, unravel, reframe, rewrite, align and enlighten the mind.

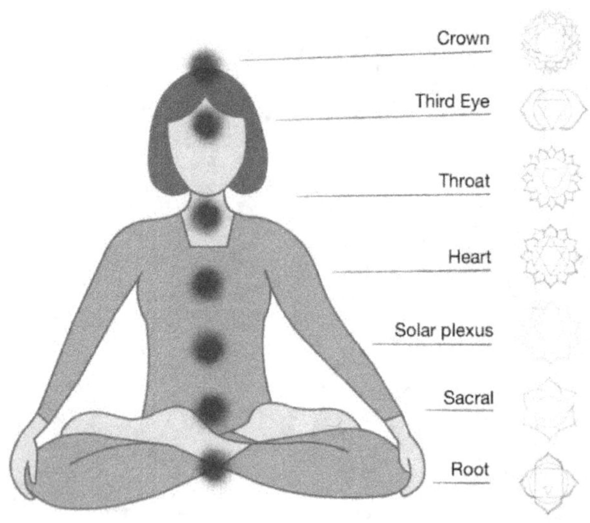

Sunset

When the Sun sets,
it does not leave us
to a life of darkness.
We become the ones
hiding behind the Moon,
waiting for happiness,
waiting for the shadows
to clear
when we should
bask in the sunshine
when it's here
and dance when
circling the Sun,
before the day is done.

Sonya Bhalla

Reframe

I love the concept
of retraining our brain.
There's so much to gain
by reframing our approach.

Learning to coach
ourselves to change our views;
to work through
our problems and use new tools.

Shifting our mindset
in a positive way,
keeping harmful
patterns at bay.
Reframing how we
react,
what we feel,
think, act, say,
and behave.

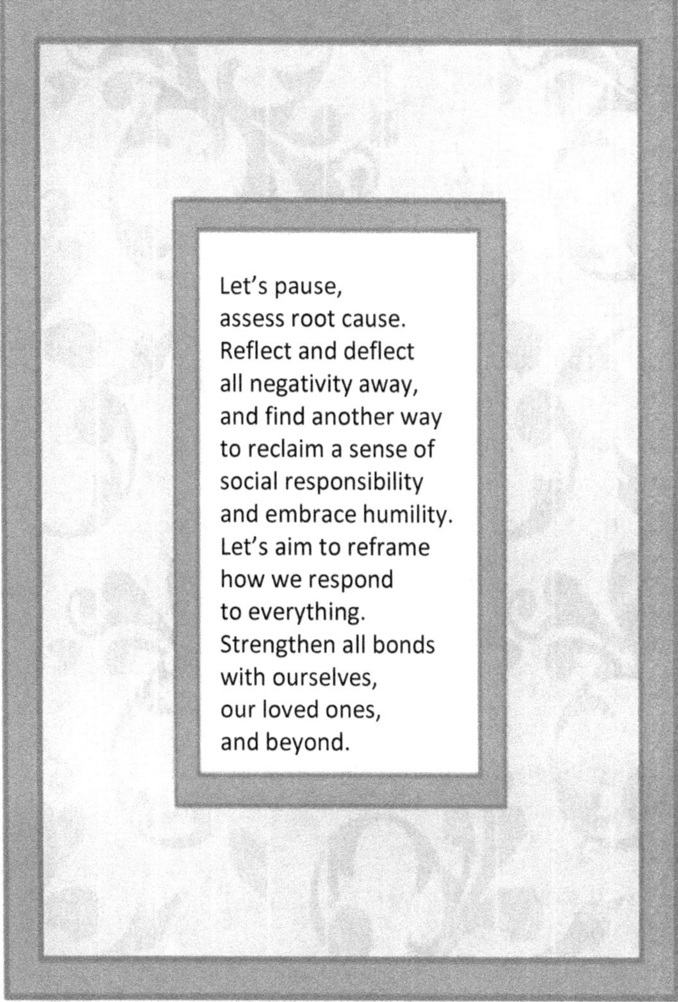

Let's pause,
assess root cause.
Reflect and deflect
all negativity away,
and find another way
to reclaim a sense of
social responsibility
and embrace humility.
Let's aim to reframe
how we respond
to everything.
Strengthen all bonds
with ourselves,
our loved ones,
and beyond.

Sonya Bhalla

Layers

In order to heal,
peel back the layers
of your auric field.

A layered spectrum
to reveal
what is concealed.

The real inner world of you
radiates outwards
a depth of view.

Layer by layer,
they're yours to unravel.
To understand
how you channel
what you feel,
what elements
you need to recover,
and to discover
your vibrant appeal.

Life is a Stage

If the script is not sensitive
to your plight
encourage the playwright
to rewrite the narrative
and support your fight.

Sonya Bhalla

Russian Dolls

A set of seven
colourful dolls
standing
side by side;
like disjointed
chakra wheels
lost and
misaligned.

Placed in a row,
ready to heal.
Each figurine
opened
to reveal
sleepy hollow
circles inside.

Balance yet
to be applied
to awaken
the mind.

Different sizes
slotting together
one by one
to harmonise,
to synthesise.

A stacking process
to stir the flow of
energy and
consciousness.

Channelling spiritual
awareness to
restore dormant
meridians.

A newfound
quotidian ritual
to find
inner peace
and clear the mind.

An intricate set
of nesting dolls
now complete
and realigned.

Abundant Affirmations

- ✓ I am enough
- ✓ I am resilient and tough
- ✓ I am present in the here and now
- ✓ I believe there's enough resources to go around
- ✓ I help and serve others with a generous heart
- ✓ I feel my joyful mindset sets me apart
- ✓ I believe in endless possibilities
- ✓ I attract progressive opportunities
- ✓ I'm inspired to think creatively
- ✓ I'm determined to live positively
- ✓ I interact with one and all with a humble attitude
- ✓ I fill my heart with immense gratitude
- ✓ I am worthy of love from everyone, including me
- ✓ I resonate at a higher frequency
- ✓ I exude love, laughter, and light
- ✓ I live a complete and fulfilling life
- ✓ I easily manifest all my desires
- ✓ I know a beautiful life is mine to acquire
- ✓ I experience my life mindfully
- ✓ I am committed to living my life abundantly

Manifesting Wishes

In my version of sleeping beauty
you are the (k)night
which can rescue my dreams
and make them a reality.

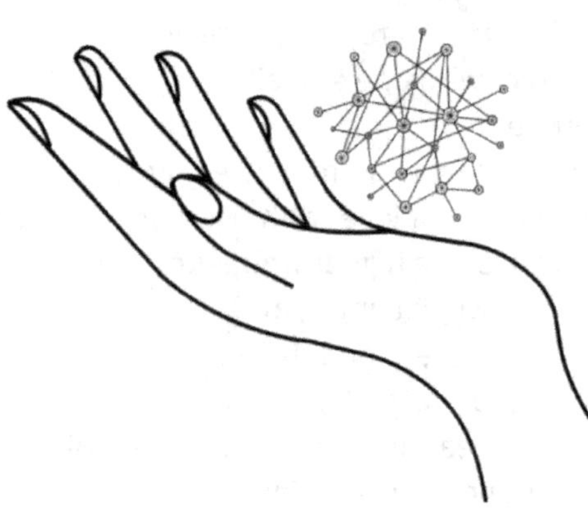

Enlighten

Be your own brand.
Your own kind of beautiful.
Let your horizons expand
so your aura's plentiful.

Be one of a kind,
let your inner beauty shine,
unwind, unbind,
and enlighten your mind.

AUTHOR'S NOTE

"If we look at the path, we do not see the sky.
We are earth people on a spiritual journey to the stars.
Our quest, our earth walk, is to look within,
to know who we are,
to see that we are connected to all things,
that there is no separation, only in the mind."
Native American

I would like to thank you for reading my poetry collection and for joining me on this journey of inner discovery.

I hope you enjoyed reading it as much as I enjoyed writing it.

We are on a continuous path of self-awareness, development and spiritual enrichment.

Of course, many things are evidence-based like science and law, and I was one such sceptic for a long time until I started to question many things and seek answers. Time and time again, there's been an innate sense that there is so much we feel, or intuitively believe is possible, without any physical evidence. Perhaps one day we will discover the truth of life, death, our true existence and our purpose.

Until then, may my musings resonate, motivate and instil a positive journey and encourage an inquisitive mind.

For more inspiration, and to see my poetry posters, please feel free to follow my Instagram page @positive.poetry.posters

Best wishes,

ABOUT THE AUTHOR

Sonya Bhalla is author and illustrator of *Enlighten,* her debut book of poetry. This collection, a labour of love over many years, is the culmination of exploring themes within her life experiences. Sonya ponders many of the universal questions we have in our lifetime and shares her musings in her inspiring writing centred around themes of self-awareness, self-development, spiritual alignment, healing, and beyond.

Sonya feels her divine purpose is to inspire others to appreciate and enrich their lives by sharing her writing with the world.

Sonya, born in England, UK, is a lawyer and mother of three wonderful children. Her favourite pastime is to write whenever time permits on scraps of paper, notebooks, apps on her phone or laptop. She has even been known to scribble on the back of receipts to capture any fragment of word wisdom, anytime, anywhere. She also loves the cinema, watching documentaries, reading, travelling, and spending time with family and friends.

Sonya draws random patterns while she thinks and finds art a relaxing medium for unwinding at the end of a long week.

She believes that we all have the power to live, love, laugh, and lift ourselves and others in a positive way, and that life itself is a journey of art and heart.

Sonya has other publications including the Global Gems Series, A to Z series and other books.

This book is published by Sonya Bhalla under the Published Printing & Text Permit issued by the Ministry of Culture and Youth (MCY) under number MC-01-01-0914975. The age group to which the content of the book is appropriate according to the age classification system issued by the Emirates Media Council is E.